The S.P.E.A.R. Paradigm

Encountering God

BRIAN L. EVANS

*R*apier
PUBLISHING COMPANY

The S.P.E.A.R. Paradigm
Encountering God

Copyright © 2018 Brian L. Evans
ISBN 978-1-946683-24-3
Library of Congress Control Number 2019938192

Published by

Rapier Publishing Company

Dothan, Alabama

www.rapierpublishing.com

First Edition

Printed in the United States of America

Book Cover Design: Garrett Myers/ Book Layout: Rapture Graphics

The views expressed in this work are solely those of the author and do not necessarilary reflect the views of the publisher. The publisher hereby disclaims any responsibilities for them.

Then he asked them, "But who do you say I am?" Simon Peter answered, "You are the Messiah, the Son of the living God. Jesus replied, "You are blessed Simon son of John, because my Father in heaven has revealed this to you. You did not learn this from any human being.
Matthew 16:15-17 (NLT)

There has been a paradigm shift in the world of Christianity. Only those who are sensitive to the heart of God can perceive this shift. In this shift a new breed of Christians has evolved. Many of these worshipping warriors were once wounded and left to die on the battlefield of ministry, but God, never leaving or forsaking them, searched and rescued them, and is now restoring them to their rightful position in Him. These once battlefield-ridden soldiers are armed with new knowledge and wisdom from the Holy Spirit to impact and influence their generation. They are poised to do great exploits, because they "know their God" (Daniel 11:32).

In the S.P.E.A.R. Paradigm, author Brian Evans, presents a pattern for assuming the posture of the worshipping warrior, thereby, preparing the mature God-Seekers for an authentic experience with God. The result is knowing God how he originally intended to be known. The S.P.E.A.R. Paradigm teaches one how to recover from a "faith collapse" by employing the "Three C's" (context, continuity, and condition) of promise interpretation, how to enter into the presence of God through the "Five Porticos" of prayer, and finally, how to maintain a daily attitude of worship by embracing the "God Paradox." Prepare for a paradigm shift…prepare to encounter God!

S.——-Spend Time With God
P.——-Ponder The Scriptures
E.—Expect An Encounter
A.—Align With God's Will
R.—Release The Love Of God

Acknowledgments

Holy Father, thank you for your inexhaustible love. I acknowledge you as the one who has given me the will to live again. Thank you for the strength to complete this first work of many more to come.

To Pete and Fannie Pierce, along with the Rapier Publishing family, thank you for believing in me and my vision enough to publish my voice. We did it!!!!! I now live in the manifestation of the prophetic words that you spoke over my life. I am eternally grateful for your life-giving encouragement and mentorship as I walked through the writing (and rewriting) process. I am eternally grateful.

To my parents, Lonnie and Gale Evans, I love you immensely. Thank you for your never-ending love, support and prayers, as I rambled on and on about this book. I literally would not be here if it were not for you.

To my sister, Janet Evans, I love you more than you know. I am grateful for your prayers and for the anointing that is evident on your life.

To my brother and sister, Reggie and Kendra Lyas, if only I were as amazing as you both make me feel…I love you. Thank you for providing a safe space for me to heal under the auspices of your unconditional love.

To my pastors, Shomari and Jacque White, thank you for restoring my faith and trust in the pastoral office. I have no doubts that your prayers helped to bring me back to life. You both are the inspiration for many of the words contained within these pages. I am honored to serve under your leadership and tutelage.

To Derrick and Tavia Jackson, Brandon and Michelle Tillman, and Larrissa Scruggs, you guys are my lifeline. Thank you for the time and effort that you all invested into my vision. Your friendship has taught me the value of accountability.

To Alan Young, thank you for seeing more in me than I see

in myself. You have no clue how much you push me out of my comfort zone. Thank you for sharing your platform with me, and providing a space for me to share my story. I am humbled to be a part of your story.

To Sy Nance, you have been such a vital part of the progression of this work. Thank you for being my coach through this process. Thank you for the wealth of knowledge that you have imparted into me, and for not letting me quit.

Table Of Contents

Introduction

Does God exist? If he does, how do we interact with him? I do not believe it is beyond my reach to assume we all have at some point wrestled with these two questions during our tenure on Earth. How we answer the first question will determine how we grapple with the second. In other words, our ability to truly know God demands a genuine forsaking of ourselves and what we claim to understand about him. One may ask from whence comes the origin of my audacious claim that one can "know" God. To that person, I say, let us examine the finer nuances of knowledge as it relates to perception and intimacy.

I submit that it is indeed possible to have contact with someone and totally not perceive or recognize who they really are. Let me validate this statement. In Luke 24, after his resurrection, Jesus appeared to two of his followers as they travelled from Jerusalem to Emmaus. The journey was about seven miles. As they walked, Jesus engaged with them through a peculiar interaction about the news headlines of the day...Jesus goes missing from the tomb after being crucified. I can imagine that was the topic of discussion amongst the natives. As they approached the town, Jesus began to drop some serious revelation on them, to the point where they forbade him to leave. The entire time they were walking together, they had no clue that the man talking to them was indeed the Savior. It wasn't until Jesus' communal gesture of breaking bread at dinner and serving them that they recognized who he was. The moral of this story is, you will never really know who Jesus is until you daily sit at his feet and dine in his presence. They literally walked seven miles with Jesus not knowing who he was. I wonder how many miles we have walked with him without recognizing who he really is and what he is to us.

The original intent of this book is not to convince the reader of the existence of God. Rather, it assumes the first question has been settled, and the answer is a resounding "YES...God does exist." This book was written to obliterate the religious cages that have been designed to contain the Almighty. He cannot be contained within the confines of our understanding and perceptions, and any attempt to do so grossly veils the true power of knowing him. In essence, our inability to understand God, in no way influences our ability to know and love him.

From this perspective, we will together grapple with the second question and that is: How do we interact with such an awe-inspiring God? Better yet, how has God providentially interacted with us from eternity? Since our belief has been concretized in the existence of God, the responsibility lies upon us to actively cultivate our belief in him, thereby setting the stage for an authentic experience with God. Questions like these are indeed daunting considerations. However, if our desire is to cross the chasm of mediocrity, how we answer these two questions will be our bridge. As we travail in the pursuit of building our bridges, think it not strange or shocking when the corpses of good intentions slain by the comfort of mediocrity begin to come into view. These are they who ran well, but were unable to successfully summon the self-discipline required to endure the course. We all must die. However, God in his mercy has afforded us the opportunity to choose how we die. Either we will die to our carnal desires in the refining fires of God's crucible, or we will die by yielding to the flesh and its inevitable course of corruption. Ultimately, the choice is ours. Moses stated in Deuteronomy 30:19 (KJV), *"I call heaven and earth to record this day against you, that I have set before you life and death, blessing and cursing: therefore choose life, that both thou and thy seed may live."*

This day, I echo the voice of Moses as I present a paradigm that seeks to open a new portal of thought regarding knowing and experiencing God. A paradigm that seeks to violently overthrow and burn to the ground the old, decaying institutions of religious pomp and circumstance. The impotent institutions that have denied the true power of God as stated in 2 Timothy 3:5. Like fig trees that have leaves but no figs, clouds that never drop rain, and semen that never impregnates the womb, these institutions have left us malnourished, hungry, and barren. It is time for a paradigm shift.

The S.P.E.A.R. Paradigm is a product of my journey as a God-obsessed truth seeker. The times and the seasons of my life have been captured and chronicled for all to learn and benefit from my failures, disappointments, rebellion, repentance, and revelation. I will be the first to quickly admit that my name is not laden with the credentials of any particular educational merit. What I am laden with is the burden to share my faith in love by the authority of Jesus Christ and his revealed truth. His love rescued me from the jaws of death, and my hope is to throw out a lifeline to anyone who may be engaged in similar struggles.

My story begins in 1999, with an experience that I have coined the faith collapse. I define a faith collapse as a rebelling against God induced by a devastating collision between God's will and ours. In other words, a faith collapse is when we walk away from God because he didn't perform how we wanted him to. There are times when our will and God's will collide. Our initial encounter with this phenomenon creates cracks in the foundation of our faulty belief systems, creating an eruption of despair and confusion. So often, God is the target of our blame, and in our enflamed ignorance, we act out based on a masterfully crafted lie. As we mature and grow in wisdom, we learn to recognize these opposing "collisions" of wills, and quickly realign and submit to God's sovereignty. If we expect to benefit in the long term, it is imperative that God be declared the winner in these skirmishes of the wills.

Leading up to my faith collapse was a series of very unfortunate events that happened within a very short time period. The death of a beloved family member, the loss of my job at a prominent communications company, combined with a very nasty divorce, left me feeling broken beyond repair. Keep in mind, I was operating in ministry and faithfully plugged in at my church during the course of all of these events. Words cannot express the level of pain that was surging through my being in that season. I was convinced that God hated me and had totally forsaken me. When I attempted to pray, God was painfully silent. I felt like Chris in the movie *"Get Out"* when he was hypnotized and falling deeper and deeper into a bottomless abyss in spite of every attempt to fight the fall.

Things in my life continued to grow progressively worse until I reached the point where I began to lose the will to live. I vividly remember the exact moment I decided to give up and walk away from God. One day, as I was leaving the attorney's office after filing for divorce number one (yes…I am twice divorced), I distinctly remember sinking into this deep pit of despair and hopelessness. That's when I simply said, "I'm done." It was a quiet resolve, nothing earth-shattering. At that very moment, I simply decided to give up. I was done with church, I was done with the "saints," and I was done with God. I was so angry with him for silently sitting by and allowing these things to happen to me. My life was a wreck, and each day I felt pieces of myself falling away. At that point I didn't care about doing the right thing anymore. Church, God, and everything I had learned in church were enemies to me now. My decision eventually led to me questioning the very existence of God. I had erroneously indicted God and found him guilty of failing me. My pain became my gavel. I blamed God for everything. Sundays would roll around, and I would roll over in my bed. This became my new normal. As I look back in the rear-view mirror of my life during this time, I now understand that this falling away was a gradual process. Little by little, the pain intensified with each devastating life blow, and because I suppressed the pain under the guise of being "strong," it compounded. The enemy is so subtle. He uses our desire for comfort against us and gradually rocks us into a deep sleep. In C.S. Lewis' book, *The Screwtape Letters*, a master demonic tempter named Screwtape is writing a letter to his apprentice and nephew (Wormwood) providing instructions concerning how to draw a Christian man away from God. Of course, this is a fictional account, but there is one section that I found particularly interesting and significant. Screwtape writes:

> *"It does not matter how small the sins are, provided that their cumulative effect is to edge the man away from the Light and out into the Nothing. Indeed, the safest road to Hell is the gradual one—the gentle slope, soft underfoot, without sudden turnings, without milestones, without signposts."*[1]

I gradually drifted into a dangerous place of apathy because I gave my pain the microphone, and it spoke louder than the still, soft voice of God's unconditional love for me. I felt like God had let me down, and that hopelessness left me contemplating suicide multiple times. Fortunately, I didn't have the gall to carry out the act. I can't fully explain why I could never find the courage to do it. All I know is at this very moment, I'm so happy I didn't. Pain creates the illusion that what is happening in the present moment will never end. This is the lie that must be eradicated by the knowledge of the love of God. To know God is to know that he doesn't strike us down even when we lash

---

1. C. S. Lewis, The Screwtape Letters, (New York, NY: Harper One, 1942), p. 25.

out against him. He is patient and longsuffering toward us, constantly drawing us to himself. "The Lord hath appeared of old unto me, saying, Yea, I have loved thee with an everlasting love: therefore, with lovingkindness have I drawn thee." Jeremiah 31:3 (KJV). God is never far from us. He may grow silent in order to grow us up, but in no way will he ever forsake us. He promised to never leave us or forsake us. We have his word.

As I sank deeper into rebellion, I began to embrace the concept that I was no longer a Christian. I started entertaining agnosticism and even opened myself up to atheistic ideology. I developed an insatiable appetite for atheistic ideas and debate. I sought out influential atheists such as the late Christopher Hitchens and Sam Harris in order to study their viewpoints refuting the existence of God. The arguments appealed to my intellect, so because I couldn't make sense of the silence of God, I used intellect and logic to refute His existence. I would intentionally seek out Christians for debate, because it was entertaining to me. I discovered that many Christians didn't know why they believed what they professed. I found pleasure in watching their faces as the confusion set in while I injected all of my atheistic venom. I became the enemy.

Looking back, I cringe when I think of the things I did in that phase of my life. Thank God my turning point came in 2005. While I was making a pharmaceutical sales call at a local physician's office in a small Florida town called Graceville, God changed my whole life. The day started off like any other, and as I walked into this small practice, I was escorted back to speak with the physician about my products. Little did I know, this physician was a born-again Christian. Shortly after I was taken to a narrow hallway to wait for the physician, he exited one of the patient rooms. When he saw me waiting, he started to approach me. We greeted each other, and I began my spiel. All of a sudden, right in the middle of my detail, he asked me if I was born again. Of course, this completely caught me off guard, but I recovered quickly. Knowing what the politically correct answer was to this question, I boldly answered, "Yes, I am," despite the fact I knew I was living in a backslidden state. The physician quickly discerned my hypocrisy and immediately began to prophesy to me right there in the hallway. I still get chills to this day just thinking about it. He proceeded to tell me that I had been involved in some very vile behavior, and God was demanding that I return to him. At that moment, he escorted me into an empty patient room and laid hands on me and rebuked the enemy. Immediately, the chains that had me shackled fell away, and I was instantly set free. When I got up off the floor, and was able to walk again, I knew I had encountered the true and living God.

As I returned to my car and continued to collect myself, I was literally in awe of what God had done. There in my car, with tears in my eyes, I heard the voice of God speak to me once again after such a long time of drought. His still voice told me to look up. As I raised my head, I noticed the signage on the face of the physicians practice building, and it read, Graceville Family Medicine. As I stared at the sign, God spoke to me clearly saying he had ordered my steps and brought me to Graceville, Florida by His GRACE which is sufficient for me. God's grace is truly amazing!!!

My reason for sharing this story is to contrast two opposing perceptions of God at varying times in my life. The truth of who God is never changed, but my perception and what I believed about him did. Jesus stated in John 14:6 (KJV), *"I am the way, the truth, and the life: no man cometh to the Father but by me."* The truth never evolves because there is no need for it to change. It simply stands in its place, and waits to be discovered. Our beliefs may shift, but truth remains constant. The earth has always been round, even when it was believed to be flat. It was only after the work of astronomers and philosophers, such as Aristotle and Eratosthenes, that the round earth theory was adopted as truth. Moral of the story…beware of the vox populi. Many times, truth runs contrary to popular belief, and beliefs are not easily changed. They are often entrenched and encased in the inertia of habit, and can only be changed by new information and experiences. Enter the S.P.E.A.R. Paradigm!

In our journey together we will explore this paradigm as we examine the five transformative disciplines listed below:

S.——-Spend Time With God
P.——-Ponder The Scriptures
E.——Expect An Encounter
A.——Align With God's Will
R.——Release The Love Of God

Four of the five disciplines happen internally. I believe God has designed us to operate from a place of wholeness and overflow. Before we can live in a place of significance, we must be whole beings. Not until we are truly filled can we expect to become fruitful. Not until we are truly healed can we expect to become helpful. Chinese philosopher, Lao Tzu once stated, "A journey of a thousand miles begins with a single step."

CHAPTER 1

S.P.E.A.R.

Spend Time with God (The Prayer Habit)

"For it is God which worketh in you both to will and to do of his good pleasure,"
Phillippians 2:13 (KJV)

The first order of business as we set out on our journey to encounter God is to understand his nature. What is God like? This is a loaded question, and one that will never be completely answered in our lifetime. Simply put, God lives outside of our intellectual reach and our capacity to comprehend. He is in a class by himself, and there is absolutely no one like him. He has no equal. He is the Supreme Being who sits in eternity and observes time. All of our efforts to understand or even describe him are hopelessly futile. He transcends all human comprehension and thought, thus raising the first obstacle in our pursuit of him. In fact, the title of this chapter is its own paradox because God lives in eternity, which is a foreign concept to all creation since we are bound by the illusion that we call time. How can we contact a Being who lives outside of the confines of time, or how can we, who, exists in the limitations of time access eternity? Is there some type of cosmic bridge that connects our worlds and states of existence thus affording us opportunities for communion together? To answer these questions is the goal of this chapter as we examine the first discipline of the S.P.E.A.R. Paradigm: Spend Time with God.

The God-Craving

Spending time with God in prayer requires a unique type of discipline that can be daunting to the average person. In order to be successful in this discipline, there must be a drive deep within us to pursue God even when we don't "feel" like it, or we don't see immediate results. The good news is this drive can be developed over time as we consistently press into our daily prayer habit. Things may seem a little awkward at first, but as we persist in our pursuit, something extraordinary happens. Our spirits begin to crave God's presence.

Have you ever experienced a craving that seemingly came out of nowhere? This often occurs when we crave our favorite foods. For an example, when I was a child, I was exposed to what I consider to be one of the great wonders of culinary creation...the Krispy Kreme donut. The first time I sank my teeth into this sweet circle of life, I was in love. Since that day, I have developed a love/hate relationship with the "Hot Now" sign. Having come into the knowledge that eating a half dozen glazed donuts in one sitting is not the plan of God for my life, I have come to a resolve to limit my consumption of Krispy Kreme donuts because of a higher drive or craving. I want to live a healthy lifestyle free of many of the health complications that come with massive donut consumption. However, though I have come to this resolve, there are still times when I am hit with a monster craving for a fresh glazed donut.

As you can see, the struggle to stop craving these delectable delights is still very real for me. There is a powerful principle that I would like to lift from my struggle. And that is, what we crave is intimately tied to what we are exposed to. The question arises, if I had never been exposed to Krispy Kreme donuts, would I have a craving for them today? It is highly unlikely that

I would, seeing that I would not have a point of reference to tie my craving to. In this simplified example we can see that without initial exposure to a thing, the craving cannot exist. There is ignorance, or what we call innocence, that prevails until we are exposed to that specific thing. Thus, my exposure to donuts became the catalyst to my craving donuts.

There is a deeper revelation in this same vein that we shall now explore. The more frequently I am exposed to a specific thing, the more intense my craving becomes. When I was initially exposed to the donut the first time, I probably would have been fine without ever eating another one. However, when I was exposed to more donuts on other occasions throughout my life, I began to develop what psychologists have coined emotional linkage to the taste of donuts. The process of linkage is totally natural and part of our DNA. As I continued to indulge in eating more donuts, the circuitry of my brain began to change as the pleasure centers were activated when I ate one, thus setting the stage for the monster cravings that would follow.

How does this concept of craving apply to prayer and time with God? To answer this question, we must first examine the difference between craving a donut as opposed to craving the presence of a person. Even though these are two different pathways, one being more primal than the other, they do share similar applications. Both cravings are birthed from exposure, but the donut craving is more of a physiological phenomenon as opposed to longing for one's presence. Longing for a person is the result of relationship and the value placed on that person. There is a deeper level of desire and yearning to experience who that person is and the value they add to us when we are in their presence. There is a joining together of sorts as we commune with that person bringing joy and fulfillment. In essence, not only do we long for that person, but we long for who we become when we are in the presence of that person.

This is the foundation for our relationship with the Father. Our longing for him transcends other fleshly desires and brings us to a place of existence outside of the limitations of the carnal. Our moments of prayer bring us to a place outside of our current location in time, as we cross the bridge into the eternal. Perhaps the most powerful aspect of engaging with God in prayer is realizing that he is the reason we desire him in the first place. He births within us a desire to interact with him. In his timeless classic, *"Mere Christianity,"* one of my favorite authors, C. S. Lewis describes our act of prayer in this way:

> *"An ordinary simple Christian kneels down to say his prayers. He is trying to get into touch with God. But if he is a Christian he knows that what is prompting him to pray is also God: God, so to speak, inside him. But he also knows that all his real knowledge of God comes through Christ the Man who was God—that Christ is standing beside him, helping him to pray, praying for him. You see what is happening. God is the thing to which he is praying—the goal he is trying to reach. God is also the thing inside him which is pushing him on—the motive power. God is also the road or bridge along which he is being pushed to that goal. So that the whole threefold life of the three-personal Being is actually going on in that ordinary little bedroom where an ordinary man is saying his prayers. The man is being caught up into the higher kinds of life—what I called Zoe or spiritual life: he is being pulled into God, by God, while still remaining himself."*[2]

The essence of prayer is captured perfectly in these words. If it were not for this truth, there would be no relationship be-

---

2. C. S. Lewis, *Mere Christianity*, (New York, NY: Harper One, 1952), p. 163.

tween God and man, thus we would be totally and utterly lost. Unless God chooses to reveal himself to us, we cannot begin to even understand what it takes to approach him. When we pray, we may not "feel" anything at all, but the entire God-head is at work within us simultaneously. God is at work within us pulling us into his own presence through his own Spirit and the blood of Jesus Christ, who is the bridge upon which we travel to get to God himself. It is what Paul was conveying to the Corinthians when he penned: *"And all things are of God, who hath reconciled us to himself by Jesus Christ, and hath given to us the ministry of reconciliation...,"* 2 Corinthians 5:18 (KJV). We see then, essentially it is God who creates the desire and the longing deep within us for himself. The creator of the craving is also the object of that craving. He initiates the exposure to himself, thereby, initiating our encounter with him. Our responsibility is to never resist him, and to always avail ourselves to him when he calls.

Mixed Signals

Identifying this God-craving can be very complex and, needless to say, very confusing. Many times, people confuse the craving for God with the craving for other things, and in turn, attempt to satisfy those cravings with carnal substitutes. Some time ago, I enrolled in a weight loss program to lose a few pounds. As part of that program, I was told to drink plenty of water throughout the day, at least eight glasses to be exact. This was a lifestyle change for me because I didn't like drinking water. I would drink the bare minimum each day. I later learned this was not good because if I was ever on the verge of dehydration, my body would send a signal to my brain in the form of a craving. Sometimes this craving would be interpreted as a craving for food, but in essence it would be my body's way of saying, "Hey Brian...I'm dying of thirst here, Bro. I need H2O." It wasn't until I actually started drinking enough water each day that I realized what I thought was hunger was actually thirst.

Tragically, many people seek to satisfy the God-craving with other, more addictive substances not fully understanding that exposure leads to cravings. I believe this is how addiction finds a foothold in our lives. According to the Addiction Center website, approximately 50 million people are addicted to tobacco products including cigarettes, cigars, chewing tobacco, and snuff.[3] Of those who smoke 90% started before the age of 18. These numbers really prove the power of cravings, and how we structure our lives around supporting these cravings. Addiction is nothing more than a craving that has no "off" switch. It is the way we seek to satisfy a persistent, never-ending longing for something we have been exposed to repeatedly. The problem with addiction is the physiological changes that take place in our brains each time we indulge. With each indulgence, a greater, more voracious appetite is created. It really is a pretty clever trap. Addiction attaches to a perfectly natural desire or drive, and becomes a parasitic monster that robs us of our life force.

A recent law enforcement sting called Operation Full Armor flushed out and charged thirty-eight online child predators with seeking to have sex with underage teen girls. According to a news article, (www.thestate.com),[4] law enforcement officers pretending to be young girls ages 13 to 14, sought out people who were seeking to engage in sexual activities with them via online platforms such as Craig's List. Many of those arrested were previous sex offenders, and one was even a correctional

---

3. https://www.addictioncenter.com/nicotine/

4. David Travis Bland. "Real Monsters Charged in investigation of online child predators, Sheriff Lott Says. www.thestate.com/mews/local/crime/article215572485.html: The State, July 26, 2018.

officer. What would drive these individuals to engage in such acts knowing the consequences that could ensue? It's the same thing that causes drug overdoses and extramarital affairs…the cravings.

Sin and Exposure to God

You may be asking, "If cravings are created by exposure, when were we ever exposed to God for this craving for him to be initiated in the first place?" Let me answer your question. Long ago in eternity, we existed with God in his providential fore-knowledge. In simple terms, before we were actually born we existed in God. Of course, we existed in a totally different form and in a different realm before being conscious of either. Notice how God informs Jeremiah the prophet of this truth, *"Before I formed thee in the belly I knew thee; and before thou camest forth out of the womb I sanctified thee, and I ordained thee a prophet unto the nations,"* Jeremiah 1:4-5 (KJV). Here in these verses, we get a glimpse into the providential sovereignty of God. In eternity past, God was intimately acquainted with us. We were in relationship with God before we actually knew him. We are born with an innate "knowing" that tells us in very vague terms that we were once with God. We are born searching for him. He placed a longing for himself inside of us that can only be quenched and satiated by being in his presence. Could it be that our existence on Earth today is God's answer to a problem or void that needed to be filled at this very moment in history with the miracle of our very existence? What if God, in his infinite wisdom, waited until this specific time to birth us into the earth as a solution to that specific problem or void? Your gifts, talents, strengths and even your weaknesses could all be part of a phe-nomenal solution to a complex problem that only you can solve.

The powerful thing about this exposure, is when we finally do encounter God and truly connect with him, we are instantly reminded of what it was like when we were with him in eternity. Sadly, our carnal nature can blind us and prevent us from seeking these types of encounters with God because sin has so corrupted our view of God and our perception of how God sees us. Remember in the Garden of Eden after Adam and Eve had sinned, they hid from God when they heard his voice. This is the first account of the effects of sin and what it does not only to our perception of God, but how we think he sees us. This is why living a life that pleases him is paramount if we are to experience the benefits and joy of being in the presence of God. When we sin, it doesn't change the truth of God's nature. He desires communion with us regardless of our past sins because his presence is our provision to deal with our sins. However, when we do sin, our tendency is to avoid him because how we see God has a lot to do with how we see ourselves. Our perception is how we view all of life. What we believe to be true often becomes the truth for us. Our perceptions can become almost like self-fulfilling prophecies, because we behave in ways that are in accord with our beliefs and perceptions. On many occasions we interact with people based on the lens through which we view ourselves, and if unrepentant sin has clouded our vision, we will find ourselves continually stumbling in darkness.

I believe God created us with a specific intention in his mind. Nothing about God is random. It may seem random and meaningless to us, but rest assured God is intentional in everything that he does. One morning in my time with God, he revealed to me that prayer is like looking into a mirror. His presence is like a mirror reflecting his nature, his love, and most of all his intention for us. Since we were exposed to him before we were born, prayer is the vehicle that brings us to the place of remembrance as we gaze into the mirror of his glory. My prayer to the Father is that he would allow us to see the reflection of his intention for us as we daily gaze into the perfection of his presence in prayer.

What is God like?

Developing and maintaining a God-craving takes a level of sustained, disciplined effort. Due to our sinful natures our ability to know God is severely handicapped. Consequently, if we desire to know what God is like, we must endure the painful journey of distancing ourselves from the antagonistic nature we were born with. Everything about our carnal mentality resists God and his perfectly designed will for our lives. Paul expressed this so eloquently in Romans when he stated, *"For to be carnally minded is death; but to be spiritually minded is life and peace. Because the carnal mind is enmity against God: for it is not subject to the law of God, neither indeed can be,"* Romans 8:6-8 (KJV). In light of this truth, the first order of business is to somehow renounce the rebellious nature of our flesh and move in the opposite direction toward the things that please God. Knowing this is half the battle, because it arms us with the mentality of a soldier as we fight the enemy of our carnal mindset. Think of it this way, we must rebel against our own rebellion. As we distance ourselves from this mindset of rebelling against God's best for our lives, we begin to come into the knowledge of truth, and our desire to align with it overrides our desire to rebel against it. As we learn truth, we open ourselves to the very nature of God.

I believe God has given us, as true seekers, the ability to know and interact with him. In order to cultivate a passionate relationship with the Father, there are three fundamental truths about the nature of God we must keep in mind:

1. God desires to be discovered
2. God desires to be close
3. God desires to give

To the extent to which we accept and understand these truths, will be the extent that God reveals more of himself to us. Salvation through the blood of Jesus is the right of every living person who has ever walked the face of the earth. True intimacy and the revealed nature of God is reserved only for those who have chosen to renounce the enemy of the carnal mind.

God Desires to be Discovered

God always initiates the first move in our direction. He gives us the proverbial "nudge" in our inner being to test our response and our sensitivity. He stands at our heart door and knocks to see if we answer. This may happen in a church service, while engaging in a conversation, or maybe even while we are sleeping in a dream. God is always tugging at us in some form waiting for us to give him access to all areas of our lives. Whether we acknowledge it or not, we are all familiar with that knock. It can be an uncomfortable knock if we are living in a sinful disposition, and for many of us, that's why the door remains closed to him. However, God in his mercy, and because of his loving nature, he continues to knock. John brings this aspect of God's nature to light in Revelation, *"Behold, I stand at the door and knock: if any man hear my voice, and open the door, I will come in to him and will sup with him and he with me,"* Revelation 3:20 (KJV). According to Strong's Concordance, the word "sup" in this verse means to dine, or to take the principle (or evening) meal. It denotes the picture of two people sharing in a most blissful and intimate contact. When we allow God into our lives, there is no need to supply anything but the open door. He brings the meal with him. He supplies our every need in the fullness of his presence. A perfect picture of this truth is seen after the resurrection of Jesus when he appeared to his disciples as they were on the sea of Tiberias fishing. They had been out all night and caught nothing. The morning that followed, Jesus called out to them from the shore and asked them had they caught any fish. Their reply to him was "No." That's when he told them to cast their nets on the other side of the ship, and when they did, they caught over a hundred and fifty fish. When this happened, they rushed ashore and found Jesus waiting for them with some fish ready to start the cookout (John 21:1-13). The very things that we are working so hard to obtain, Jesus already has them prepared for us waiting to be discovered in his presence as we dine with him in prayer.

God Desires to be Close

One of my favorite modern worship songs is *"Reckless Love"* by Cory Asbury. Part of the bridge to this song flawlessly describes how God loves us and chases us:

> *"There's no shadow You won't light up*
> *Mountain You won't climb up*
> *Coming after me*
> *There's no wall You won't kick down*
> *Lie You won't tear down*
> *Coming after me,"*

God wants to be close to us in intimate communion. This is clearly evident by the sacrifice he made when he sent his Son to die for our sins while we were still sinners and enemies of his holiness. He became flesh, the very thing that resists his sovereignty to reconcile us back to himself, thus eradicating the curse that was initiated in the Garden of Eden. His love for us and desire to be close to us is so perfect that he made a special trip to Eden after Adam and Eve committed the sinful act to cover them. His perfect holiness and repulsion for sin didn't stop him from making provision for Adam and Eve. For so long we have focused on the curses that he dealt out to Adam, Eve, and the serpent that we missed the covering that he supplied. Even though the ground was cursed, it still produced, and even though God was angry with Adam and Eve, he still clothed and covered them. Even the curse of death was a demonstration of the love and mercy of God (I won't unpack this revelation here…maybe in my next book). The Bible states, "*Unto Adam also and to his wife did the Lord God make coats of skins, and clothed them,*" Genesis 3:21 (KJV). We observe one of the great truths of the nature of God in this verse. He longs to be near us even after we sin against him. The lie that God ceases to love us when we sin is another way our perception of him becomes perverted due to our carnal nature. On the contrary, this verse shows us that he longs to be near us and to cover us when we fall. If we keep pursuing God through the ups and downs of this sanctification process, we will continue to grow from one level of glory to the next according to 2 Corinthians 3:18. God responds to our pursuit of him. James 4:8 (KJV) states, "*Draw nigh to God and he will draw nigh to you.*" The faintest lean toward him initiates a response from him that bridges every chasm between him and us. He lights up the darkness and kicks down walls to get to us. In our longing for him, he longs for us. In our chasing him, he chases us. In our drawing nigh to him, he draws nigh to us. That is his nature.

God Desires to Give

Another aspect of the nature of God that we see in scripture is his desire to give to us. The cornerstone of our hope in him lies in his gift to us as written in the Gospel of John, "*For God so loved the world, that he gave his only begotten Son, that whosoever believeth in him should not perish, but have everlasting life,"* John 3:16 (KJV).

We have often limited the hand of God by only asking for materialistic accoutrements that only supply us with a false sense of security. Yes, God does supply us with these things, and he knows we need and desire them before we even ask him, but there is so much more that he desires to give to us. Greater gifts he waits to bestow to the one who dares to ask; perfect gifts. Gifts that can only be obtained by communion with him. God is the source of all goodness and perfection, and he absolutely knows how to blow our minds with his favor. We have a terrible proclivity to limit God. This becomes painfully evident as we roll off all of our shallow lists to God in prayer as if we were children sitting in Santa's lap. How much more meaningful would our prayers be if we pursued God just for the reward of hearing his voice and his heartbeat? What if the goal of our prayer time was to strip ourselves of all pretense and presumption in order to be clothed with the love and light of God's presence? My prayer is for the Father to abundantly give us only what makes us want him more.

The Five Porticos of Prayer

A portico is a porch-like structure supported by huge columns usually built to cover the entrance of a building. This is a representation of how God covers us as we enter into his presence. He is drawing us into his presence, while simultaneously covering and protecting us as we make our approach--like a portico. Prayer is all about access to the Father. When we prepare to enter into the presence of God, employing the appropriate tools can greatly enhance the prayer experience, and exponentially increase the faith of the seeker. It helps to learn how God receives us when we pray, and what he likes to hear as we approach him with our petitions. To be clear, effectual and fervent prayer, as prescribed in James 5:16, is not about getting what we ask for, rather, effective prayer is about knowing what Christ has wrought in us by his death, burial, and resurrection. We have confidence through the blood of Jesus to enter into the courts of our Father and commune with him freely.

In my pursuit of God in prayer, I have learned by trial and much error, that there are certain actions that enhance the prayer experience. I call these the Five Porticos of Prayer. They are: Approach, Acknowledgment, Alignment, Asking, and Ascription. I developed this system over time to help me get the most out of my time with God. The reason prayer is so powerful is because it is literally God at work within us. In no way is this a "formula" for prayer. Time with God should always be organic, and never programmed, like a conversation with a family member. Though the conversation may be organic, there are certain language rules that we employ when communicating with each other. These "rules" can help us access the presence of God more effectively, thereby, gaining access to the throne room of God. Let's examine these porticos together.

Approach

In the Torah (Old Testament), God was very specific about how he wanted his people to worship him. Everything had its place, and everyone honored the system of pageantry that was praise and worship. God was very specific in his directives for each person involved in the worship experience. We can even see remnants of this specificity in the Psalms as we read chapters 120-134. Named the "Songs of Degrees," or "Psalms of Ascent," they were sung during their approach as they ascended up to the holy temple.

Our approach to God in prayer should always be upward-facing, reverent, and joyful. The attitude of our heart is of utmost importance as we prepare to pray, and can greatly influence how God receives us into his presence. Much of our approach begins long before we enter into our prayer closets. Before we speak any words, our approach to God should have already commenced. To illustrate, as it relates to intimacy, it is said that foreplay between couples begins long before either of them enter the bedroom. Like these couples, our approach to God should begin in our minds and hearts long before our knees touch the floor. He should be the object of our affection. Poetry and love songs should flow from our hearts toward God every day, all day, and all throughout the day. Isaiah 26:9 paints a beautiful picture to illustrate this, *"With my soul have I desired thee in the night; yea, with my spirit within me will I seek thee early..."* May our hearts be daily enthralled with the presence of the Father.

Acknowledgement

Once we actually do hit our knees, how should we begin the conversation? I will use an illustration to answer this question. Imagine if one day you invited me to your house for dinner and I agreed to come. Once I arrived, I rang the doorbell, and went straight to the kitchen table without greeting you at the door. No "hello," no hugs, or no "thank you"...just straight to the table. How would you feel in that moment? I'm afraid that many times this is how we approach God in prayer. No acknowledgement...just straight to the "gimme-gimme-gimme."

Here, I will take liberty to consult the teachings of Jesus as we examine this portico. In Luke 11, we find Jesus responding to a request to teach his disciples to pray. Here Jesus begins the model with honor and appreciation for who God is. The words, *"Our Father which art in heaven, Hallowed be thy name...,"* (11:2, KJV) brings to light the relationship that exists between God and us his children. Our first words in prayer should always be centered on our acknowledgement of who God is to us. He is our Holy Father…separate (Holy) yet near (Father). His name is "hallowed" meaning "set apart." A better way to understand this term is to think of it in relation to the common. God is the total opposite of common. There is no one or nothing else remotely close to being like him. He is the only being of his caliber in existence…all knowing, all powerful, and present in all directions (omnipresent). The more I think about this truth, the more wonderful it becomes. Acknowledging the awe of God can draw us into his presence to immediately. Nature has this effect on me as well. When I look at the wonder and splendor of God's creation, it strikes awe inside my heart, and draws me into his presence as I acknowledge him as my creator. I stand in awe.

Alignment

The next portico that facilitates our access to God is alignment. We see this in action in Luke 11:2b (KJV), *"Thy will be done, as in heaven, so in earth."* When we pray, we submit to God's will for our lives. By submitting to God's will, we give him control over the outcome of our prayers to him. I will address this in more detail in the chapter 4-Align With God's Will. As we seek the face of God, the variances in our lives become painfully evident, as the Holy Spirit engages with us. He searches our hearts and reveals those weights, sins, and weaknesses that hinder us from climbing to higher altitudes in God (Hebrews 12:1). This alignment is uncomfortable at times because it requires us to see our reflection as we really are…no make-up and no Instagram filters.

vThough it may not feel like it, the alignment portico brings us closer to God, because it was designed to produce an attitude of repentance. This brings me to the next portico…

Asking

As we dig deeper into the truths of God's word relating to prayer, you may have noticed a pattern developing. Exactly…we haven't asked for anything yet. We have made it through three of the five porticos without lifting a single request. Though prayer is a platform most commonly used for lifting petitions to God, we find in our current study that there is so much more to seeking God than "gimme-gimme-gimme." In fact, I would like to submit that that closer we get to God, the more our selfish desires shrink in the awe of his presence. We know that we are properly reflecting his glory when we reach the portico of asking and all we want is to be transformed by his presence in our lives. This portico seamlessly follows the previous one because once we are properly aligned with God, we suddenly realize the horror and ugliness of our sinful core as we stand next to the radiant beauty of his holiness. This produces a reflex deep within us of repentance, and this is the type of asking that proves that we have had an authentic encounter with God.

In Luke 11:4, note how Jesus blends this truth into his prayer curriculum. *"And forgive us our sins; for we also forgive every one that is indebted to us."* This teaches us that we are one race (human), and we all have the stain of sin deep within the fabric of our hearts. Therefore, not only do we need forgiveness, but we must also extend forgiveness to others in the same spirit of meekness and humility. Once we have crossed the jagged frontier of our own imperfect hearts, we can then see clearly to know what to truly ask for as we have need. Prayer brings God's perspective into our field of view. In prayer, we see how God sees…with his eyes. He guides us with the compass of his perspective. *"I will instruct thee and teach thee in the way which thou shalt go: I will guide thee with mine eye,"* Psalms 32:8 (KJV).

Ascription

The fifth and final portico is the seal and confirmation that we believe God just for who he is. The root word for ascription is ascribe, meaning "to assign." The connotation is that of giving credit to someone for doing something or being someone. When we ascribe glory to God, we give him credit for what has taken place in our lives. In Matthew 6:13, we clearly see Jesus instructing us to ascribe "the kingdom, the power and the glory" to God...forever. As we ascribe these things to God, we place worth on him in worship for who he is, what he has done, and what he is capable of doing. This keeps us in alignment with God because it is indicative of our submission to his sovereignty and authority as Holy Father. It matters not the outcome of our prayers as long as we have access to his holy presence and his unceasing, steadfast love. Course of these five porticos are meant to be fluid and malleable when we are actually in prayer. There is no specific sequence to these at all. There are times when I may enter through all of these porticos, and there are times when my entire prayer is devoted to ascription, or acknowledgment. This is only a resource, not a law. So relax, and just enjoy the presence of God, because this is essentially the goal of prayer, after all.

Conclusion

When we first lace up our shoes to start our journey of forming a consistent prayer habit, the going can get pretty tough. We can blame our flesh for this. Prayer is a spiritual undertaking, and Mr. Flesh wants nothing to do with it. Think about what prayer must look like to someone on the outside looking in. We talk to an invisible presence, that doesn't respond in an audible tone. In most cases there is no immediate gratification that comes from prayer. It is no wonder why most people give up before the real benefits of prayer are realized. Yet, people who have actually developed a prayer habit seem to be able to contact God as soon as they land on their knees to pray. Why the difference? It is all about exercising our spiritual senses. Paul states in Hebrews, *"For everyone who lives on milk is doctrinally inexperienced and unskilled in the word of righteousness, since he is a spiritual infant. But solid food is for the [spiritually] mature, whose senses are trained by practice to distinguish between what is morally good and what is evil,"* Hebrews 5:13-14 (AMP). Prayer is a discipline, and discipline of any kind demands consistent practice before proficiency is gained.

In 2017, I ran my first half marathon. During my training, I would hear people talk about experiencing runners high, which is a feeling of euphoria that some people feel after a long run. This concept was extremely foreign to me because up until that point during my training, I had never experienced anything remotely close to a high. A runners low, maybe, but never a high of any kind. In fact, the only reason why I was running in the first place was because I foolishly accepted a challenge from one of my coworkers to run a half. In order to prove I was serious, I paid my entry fee and started training. As the mileage increased, and the runs got longer and longer, there were several times I literally questioned my sanity. Why did I decide to do this to myself? In spite of wanting to quit on several occasions, I kept training. Through the pain and through the fatigue, I kept running. Three miles turned into five miles. Five miles turned into seven, and seven turned into nine…still no runners high. Oddly enough, what I did experience was a gradual change of mindset. I actually started to enjoy running just for the sport. I enjoyed being outdoors seeking out new scenic places to run. I suddenly realized something about the training I was enduring. Who I was becoming was much more of a reward than crossing the finish line. The process of training was transforming me into a new person. The process taught me to push through the feeling of wanting to quit until I reached my goal. One day as I was finishing up a 10-mile run, it hit me. I finally experienced the elusive runners high, and I must say it was well worth the wait. It was like a surge of strength that magically appeared and rested on me almost like a second wind that made me want to run some more...so I kept running. It was awesome.

I wish I could say I experienced runners high every time I ran, but unfortunately, this is just not the case. In many ways developing a prayer habit is much like my training. I didn't understand why it took so long for me to experience runners high, but that didn't stop me from running. We must not allow feelings of discouragement and fatigue stop us from consistently pursuing God in prayer. P.U.S.H.-Pray Until Something Happens!!! As we create excitement around our prayer times, our prayers will become more fervent and meaningful. As we separate ourselves from sin and draw nigh to God, he will draw nigh to us. David once wrote, *"Delight thyself also in the Lord; and he shall give thee the desires of thine heart,"* Psalm 37:4 (KJV). As we delight in spending time with God, he becomes our desire. Our hearts long for him and crave the closeness of his presence. His presence becomes the reward, and as a result of this transformation, he gives us more of himself. The process of seeking him transforms us as our will harmonizes with his. We desire what he desires for us. There may be a fight before the delight, but like runners high, he is worth the fight.

CHAPTER 2

S.P.E.A.R.

Ponder the Scriptures (The Light)

*"In the beginning was the Word, and the Word was with God, and the
Word was God...In him was life; and the life was th elight of men. And
the light shineth in darkness; and the darkness comprehended it not,"*
John 1:1,4-5 (KJV)

We are creatures of light. Virtually everything we do depends on being able to see objects in space, which can only be accomplished in the presence of light. Little is known about how light is created and how it travels, but the little we do know about this electromagnetic phenomenon makes us hungry to understand more. What we do understand is there are many different classes of light radiation based on the frequencies and wavelengths at which it travels. The electromagnetic (EM) spectrum is a scientific tool used to classify the various types of light radiation and the names of each class. The most fascinating aspect of this classification is our ability to only see and perceive a small sliver of this EM spectrum. Scientists call this small sliver "visible light." This is the range of the spectrum that our eyes perceive activating our sense of sight. Our eyes are highly specialized organs designed to capture and process this light energy so that we may see the things around us. From this highly specialized ability to perceive light, we are able to make split-second decisions that could, in certain situations, mean the difference between life and death. There are people who struggle to properly process light, which leads to various issues with visual acuity, or the ability to see clearly. In fact, some of these issues can be quite limiting and can even lead to blindness.

Light and Blindness

Don't you hate when you wake up in the middle of the night because you have to use the restroom? If your experience is like mine, this always happens when I'm having the best sleep of my entire adult life, or when I am in the middle of dreaming about winning the lottery. Not long ago, I was a victim of this atrocity. Of course, the worst part of this entire event was when I had to turn on the light switch in my restroom. There was no way to prepare for the sheer rudeness of the bright light as it seared my very eyeballs. For that reason, I thought it would be a great idea to walk back to my bed in the darkness. At the time, I had the utmost confidence in my drowsy, night-walking skills. As I was clumsily making my way back to my bed, my world was rocked as my toe found the edge of the footboard. For a brief moment, my spirit left my body as the pain sent shockwaves over my entire being. Fortunately, all of my toes were still intact, but I learned a powerful lesson from that experience. That fateful night, I was reminded of the value of light. I learned the hard way that just because I cannot see an object, does not mean that object does not exist. The foot of my bed was concealed by darkness, and my eyes did not have the assistance of the light to perceive it. Consequently, in that moment, I was essentially a blind man.

Spiritual blindness is caused by an understanding deficiency. The enemy can sometimes manipulate our emotions causing us to erroneously process the events of our lives. In these moments, we have a tendency to associate pain with evil and comfort with good. When things happen to us that do not feel good, our defense mechanisms are triggered, creating spiritual blinders which can potentially block truth from penetrating our hearts. Sometimes we throw emotional tantrums when we do not get what we want. It is not until later in life when we finally realize the thing we wanted so badly, but did not obtain, was ultimately not God's best for us. Our lack of understanding creates blindness, and if we do not yield to the light of the Spirit, we may stub our toes because we are trying to walk in the dark.

Blindness occurs when something goes awry with the way our eyes capture and process light. Without waxing too scientific, sight is basically our ability to process the light that reflects off of the objects around us. Essentially, what causes us to "see" that car drive by, or that book on our coffee table, is the light that reflects off of the surfaces of those objects. Our eyes contain special cells that enable our brains to interpret the light patterns as they reflect off of the objects that we see. Blindness is the inability to properly interpret the light patterns that reflect off of the surfaces of objects, making sight difficult or impossible. When we think of a person who is blind, we may picture someone who is wearing dark sunglasses and sweeping a walking cane across the ground as they walk. While this is one image that may ring true, there are varying degrees of blindness that may not be as obvious to us.

In order for a person to be declared "legally blind," according to the National Federation of the Blind (https://nfb.org/blindness-statistics),[5] central visual acuity must be 20/200 or less in the better eye with the best possible corrective measures in place. In other words, a person who is legally blind may perceive a measure of light, but definitely not as clearly as person with normal visual acuity. For instance, they will only be able to see at 20 feet what a person with normal vision can see clearly at 200 feet (i.e., 20/200 visual acuity). This is quite staggering. Although most of us are not plagued with this level of blindness, a vast number of us may have milder cases of visual impairment. Fortunately, there are instruments that have been developed that can correct

---

5. National Federation of the Blind, (https://nfb.org/blindness-statistics).

those impairments. Corrective lenses, contact lenses, and even LASIK surgery have all afforded us the opportunity to correct our visual impairments enabling us to see clearly. Trust me, you do not want to ride with me at night if I ever have to drive without my glasses. These impairments, though small, do inconvenience us from time to time, and it all boils down to how we process light. When sin entered our world through Adam and Eve, it blinded all of us by infecting our perception of God and ourselves. Our light discerning faculties were severely handicapped, and the ability to perceive and process spiritual light was compromised. Until Jesus flipped the light switch on and redeemed us, restoring our sense of sight, we were trapped in a state of spiritual blackout. Since light is so vital from a biological perspective, let's examine how it affects us as we ponder the word of God.

Light and the Bible

The King James Version of the Bible mentions the word "light" approximately 272 times in 235 verses. Of course, not all of these refer to the word of God as being light, but there are some powerful comparisons between the word of God and light. Psalm 119:105 (KJV) states, *"Thy word is a lamp unto my feet, and a light unto my path."* As Christians, we vehemently defend the Bible as being the inspired Word of God, given for the benefit of our learning and encouragement. We believe that the Bible was written by people who walked in close proximity to God, enabling them to clearly hear and document His voice. We also believe that God inspired these people to document what He would do in the future. The books contained in the canon of the Holy Bible are accounts of these experiences had by Abraham, Noah, Moses, Joshua, Peter, Paul and a host of others. Though these accounts are breath-taking and mind-blowing, how should we interpret them for practical application today in the 21st century and beyond?

I believe as we draw closer to God, the Bible plays an important role in how we perceive the things of God. Once we engage in searching for common themes and threads throughout the Bible, our picture of what God is like begins to form and becomes clearer and clearer. Psalm 119:130 (KJV) states, *"The entrance of thy words giveth light; it giveth understanding unto the simple."* The Scriptures are our gateway to the heart of God. Reading and studying the Bible is like turning on a light switch in the spirit realm. This light reveals all of the wonderful things that we have access to, and teaches us how to employ them in our own lives. The Bible is not just an ordinary book. It contains the living energy of God's Spirit that is unleashed in us as we meditate on the words contained in it. Herein lies a perplexing dilemma. How can simple words on a page create energy and light within us just by reading and constantly thinking about them? Keep reading my friend, because that is the question that we will wrestle with for the remainder of this chapter.

Light and Faith

In March of 2017, my family and I took a much anticipated vacation to California. While there on the incomparable west coast, we were amazed at the beautiful landscapes and shorelines as we ventured into the various parts of the Golden State. One of the highlights of our trip was visiting the Muir Woods National Monument. The experience of seeing colossal redwood trees in their natural habitat was one that I will never forget. Until then, I had always desired to see them with my own two eyes, and stand next to one as it towered endlessly over me. I had seen pictures of people visiting the redwoods, and read about their experiences in the forests where these giants live. All of the pictures I had seen, and all of the stories I read, created a longing to have my own experience with these natural wonders.

When we read and study the Bible, we experience a similar type of scenario. Think of the Bible as a picture book of other people's experiences with God. From their experiences, we get to see what God is like by how He interacted and communicated with them. The Bible tells us what is spiritually possible. It teaches us how to live in a way that pleases the Father. By studying the Scriptures, a clear image of the spiritual world is superimposed on our hearts, so that we can see eternal things as the light of God's glory reflects off of them. Reading the Bible increases our capacity to experience God, and heightens our desire for eternal things. Remember in the last chapter when we discussed cravings? We increase our craving for God, by exposing ourselves to His word daily. Jesus stated in John 5:39 (KJV), *"Search the scriptures; for in them ye think ye have eternal life: and they are they which testify of me."* The scriptures tell us how God likes to interact with us. Remember, He likes to be discovered by us, He likes to be close to us, and He likes to give to us. These aspects of His nature are contained in the scriptures, and as Jesus said in John 5:39, they "testify" of him. The Greek word for testify is martyreō which means: to affirm that one has seen, heard or experienced something...(Thayers Greek Lexicon).

Going back to my California trip, seeing pictures of the mighty redwoods created an image within me that increased my desire to experience the very thing I was looking at. The photographs told a story that words could not convey alone. Through the pictures, I was able to see what the redwoods were like. I saw where they lived. The pictures gave me the conceptual knowledge that such a place existed, and although I had never actually been to this place, a "faith image" was created inside of me. Faith makes visible what was once hidden by the darkness of our own sin and ignorance. Take a look at the word "imagination." What root word do you see? If you said "image" you win! I believe God gave us the ability as humans to imagine without limitations. We even have the ability to see things that do not exist. If I tell you to imagine a pink and blue polka dot horse, wearing cowboy boots walking on the beach. We all know that animal doesn't exist, but you just created the image in your imagination, and for you, it became "visible." When we ponder and meditate on the word of God, it creates an image deep within us, and this image generates faith. Hebrews 11:1 (KJV) states, *"Now faith is the substance of things hoped for, the evidence of things not seen."*

Initially, only you can see your faith image. People may mock you and call you crazy because of what you "see," but remember, you have the advantage of light. Stop allowing people who are in darkness to speak over your life. They cannot see what you see. You have the light working in your favor, and that light gives you the power to act on the faith picture that only you can see. This is why I only share my faith pictures with people who are of like faith. Not everyone will understand your faith picture, so make up your mind to work in silence until you accomplish your goal. When you finally accomplish your goal, it will speak loudly enough for you.

Not only do we have the power of unlimited imagination, we can also revisit those images whenever we want. Now that we have the polka dot horse in our imagination, we can conjure up the image of our colorful friend any time we desire. Now, for the fun part! Imagine you are walking on the beach, and all of a sudden, in the distance, you see the polka dot horse running toward you. Now imagine the horse approaching you on the beach and saying, "Greetings, friend!!! How about a ride?" You now hop on the horse and ride off into the sunset. Though this is a very simplified illustration, it reveals a powerful principle.

Not only can we create images in our imagination, but we can interact with those images. It is possible to "see" and even interact with images in our imagination that do not exist; images that are invisible in this realm. I wonder what would happen if we spent more time gazing at positive and empowering images that we have created in our imagination. What if we created images of us living happy, healthy, and pain-free lives? What if we looked at those images on a daily basis? Is it possible to look at those images long enough in our minds, and strongly believe those images, that eventually, those same images could become our reality? Paul declared in 2 Corinthians 4:18 (KJV), *"While we look not at the things which are see, but at the things which are not seen: for the things which are seen are temporal; but the things which are not seen are eternal."*

It is possible to perceive two different realms. The word of God creates within us images of another world; a world that is more real than the one we currently live in. You may be experiencing pain now, but you can choose to create another image of a healthy you, and gaze at it daily. Imagine yourself eating healthy foods and exercising regularly, and then commit to actually doing what you are thinking about. You may be unemployed now, but you can choose to create another image of you working in a successful career, and gaze at it daily. As we ponder the word of God, it latches on to our imagination and creates images of love, power and faith. As we interact with those images, we eventually create our own reality. Where you are in life at this very moment is a result of the images you have been gazing at in your mind. Remember we must not stop there. Once we combine real-time action and corresponding tasks with those faith images, our lives begin to change in very practical and powerful ways. Faith produces action, and our actions bring powerful change. Faith without works is dead. Imagine the impossible!

Light and the Voice of God

Regardless of how much time I spent poring over other people's pictures of the giant redwoods, it could never compare to my own experience as I finally walked through the forest myself. As my family and I drove into the Muir Woods Monument, our journey began high above the forest rim as we hugged sharp hairpin turns overlooking bottomless valleys and gut-wrenching cliffs. As we stepped out of our vehicle to enter the forest, the crisp, pristine air immediately overcame me. The oxygen was so plentiful; it was as if my lungs came alive in this oxygenated utopia. Once we entered the forest, I could not even see the tops of the trees. As we continued to walk through the forest winding through trails and crossing bridges over rushing rivers coursing through the forest, we eventually reached the oldest and largest of the redwoods. Everything my pictures had testified of was true, and then some. My faith images had finally become my reality.

As we pursue God, when we will inevitably begin to crave more of him. The Bible will always be a vital part of our pursuit. God's ultimate goal in creating us was to bring us into perfect, unbroken fellowship with him. Reading the Bible is like looking at photographs. It is only a representation of what is real and possible. It tells us of things that God did within the confines of certain people's lives and experiences. If we are not careful, we can make of the Bible a proverbial box as we try to fit God into our limited understanding of the scriptures. Some of the religious elites have already made this fatal mistake, committing unthinkable atrocities in the name of God. If we are to avoid such atrocities, we must discipline ourselves to not only hear the logos of God, but also the rhema of God. When God created us, He designed us to hear His voice, free of any carnal interference. There is a deeper place in God that goes beyond mere reading the Bible. Once we tap into this place in him, we become new creatures with new minds and new values. We begin to transform into godly beings capable of reflecting the light of His glory and splendor. Paul eloquently described this truth in his second letter to the Corinthians, *"But we all, with open face beholding as in a glass the glory of the Lord, are changed into the same image from glory to glory, even as by the Spirit of the Lord,"* 2 Corinthians 3:18 (KJV). In essence, we become little walking moons. We do not possess our own light, but we were created to shine in darkness, reflecting the light that emits from the Father. John, the author of the Gospel of John, articulated it perfectly when he described John the Baptist in the following passage, *"He (John the Baptist) was not that light, but was sent to bear witness of that Light,"* John 1:8 (KJV). The more we ponder the word of God, the more we transform into the image of God. This act of meditating on the scriptures causes a spiritual metamorphosis. This transformation is the result of the logos mixing with faith in us, which produces the newness of life.

Logos is one of two words in the Bible that refers to the word of God. The second word is rhema. When studying both these words, at first glance, they seem like identical twins. However, upon further scrutiny, a slight distinction is revealed which helps our case. The word Logos entails the entirety of the written word of God in the scriptures, the whole volume of the book, so to speak. It is what has been said or uttered for the purpose of declaring God's original intent. Vine's Expository Dictionary defines logos as: a word or saying, an account which one gives by word of mouth. Usage of the word logos can be found in the following passage, *"In the beginning was the Word, and the Word was with God, and the Word was God,"* John 1:1 (KJV). Rhema, on the other hand, refers to specific scriptures that can be wielded as spiritual weapons to be used in the heat of spiritual combat. Again, Vine's Expository Dictionary denotes rhema to signify: the individual scripture which the Spirit brings to our remembrance for use in time of need. This is where we begin to understand how to hear the voice of God. Pondering the scriptures is the foundation for hearing the voice of God via rhema. Usage of the word rhema is found in the following passage, *"And take the helmet of salvation, and the sword of the Spirit, which is the word of God,"* Ephesians 6:17 (KJV).

Without the Spirit of God living in us and directing us, we will neither have the capacity to understand, nor the wisdom to execute the word of God. If the word of God is the light, the Spirit of God is the eye that perceives and processes the light, thereby making it discernable to us as we study His word. Paul declared: *"But as it is written, Eye hath not seen, nor ear heard, neither have entered into the heart of man, the things which God hath prepared for them that love him. But God hath revealed them unto us by his Spirit: for the Spirit searcheth all things, yea, the deep things of God,"* 1 Corinthians 2:9 (KJV).

Logos and rhema work together just like electricity and magnetism in the production of light radiation. Combined, they give us spiritual light so that we may discern by the Spirit of God the power and life that we have access to. The reason why we read, study, and ponder the logos daily is so that we will be able to access rhema in times of need.

Conclusion

The word is only effective if it is stored in our hearts and applied to our daily living. Having a Bible and never studying it is like carrying an empty gun. If you were ever in a situation where you needed that gun, and God forbid, one day had to pull the trigger, "click" is definitely not the sound you would want to hear. Storing scriptures in our hearts equips us with the necessary ammunition to hear rhema clearly when we need it most. The Spirit of God helps us to remember specific scriptures that apply to our situation, and meets us at our point of need. John 14:26 (KJV) states, *"But the Comforter, which is the Holy Ghost, whom the Father will send in my name, he shall teach you all things, and bring all things to your remembrance, whatsoever I have said unto you."* The word of God is our concealed weapon, perfectly forged and tempered to defeat every enemy we will ever face. Gone are the days of trembling and stumbling in the dark, when light has been made available to us. Immerse yourself in the light, and prepare for the fight. Victory is yours.

CHAPTER 3
S.P.E.A.R.

Expect an Encounter (The Visitation)

"Draw nigh to God, and he will draw nigh to you,"
James 4:8a (KJV)

If I were to list some of my favorite things to do, I would start with spending time with family, eating amazing food, and relaxing on the beach are just to name a few. Moving is definitely not on that list. Even worse then moving is calling all of the utility companies to schedule a transfer or to connect new services. Recently, when calling to set up my security system install, I was told that a technician would need to come out to run the necessary diagnostics. As the representative was completing my order, she informed me that the technician would arrive to complete my order between the hours of 8 am and 12 noon. Of course, my desire was to narrow that timeframe to avoid being held hostage by the infamous 4-hour window. Although they were not able to accommodate my request, I was told the technician would call me when he/she was on the way. This was not ideal, but it was a compromise I could live with. Since I now had a confirmed appointment, I needed to make some adjustments to my schedule so that I could be present when the technician arrived at my home. My confirmed appointment created within me a very realistic expectation, and my expectation moved me to prepare for what I was expecting. Expectation is the foundation of faith, and will be the foundation upon which I build my case for why we should expect to experience the presence of God when we diligently seek him.

Expectation Explained

The definition of "expect" according to the Merriam-Webster Dictionary is: to anticipate or look forward to the coming or occurrence of. When we speak of expectation, we must take into consideration the flaws of the human mind in order to fully understand how expectation works. In fact, as we seek to fully explain what expectation is, we often encounter the word "hope," which can be defined as follows: to cherish a desire with anticipation: to want something to happen or be true. These two words are so closely related, it can be very difficult to perceive the revelatory nuances upon first glance. In some cases, both words are even used to define the other. In this chapter, I will focus on the subtle differences in meaning between both words in regards to expecting from God.

In speaking of expectation, there must first be a foundation upon which expectation rests. Expectation differs from hope because it carries a more rigid frame. The main thrust of hope is desire, while the main thrust of expectation is action. Both expectation and hope encompass strong feelings of anticipation, but when we expect something to happen, we often invest energy and action in anticipation of receiving that specific thing. Expectation often causes our posture to change as we prepare ourselves to receive the very thing we are looking forward to. We begin to use our minds differently as we internally interact with our faith images. When we consider this, we then discover our hopes often differ from our expectations because of the information that we consume. More on this topic later, but for now, in order to strengthen my point, let's take a look at an example.

Take a moment to imagine that the Powerball Lottery has

reached an astronomical $500,000,000. You and I both buy a ticket in "hoping" to win some cash. Let's say for the purposes of this example the odds of winning are 1 in 300 million. As you and I discuss our slim chances of winning, we still express our hopes of hitting the jackpot. We talk about what we would do with the money, and how our lives would immediately change. Because the probability of winning is so slim, there is no urgency to change anything about our current lives at that point, so we both remain in a state of hope. It would be a really bad idea to purchase a new home or go on a shopping spree based on mere hopes alone. Yes, we both purchased tickets, but the purchases alone are not enough to move either of us from mere hope to expectation. Until we know the winning lottery numbers, the information we currently have is inferior and incapable of supporting major decisions such as purchasing cars and mansions.

As it relates to faith, the force at which we move from hope to expectation is directly proportionate to the quality of the information we consume and act upon. We must learn to be selective in the information we take in daily. The lack of quality information leads to bad decisions, and undesirable outcomes. It is not fair to blame God for the consequences of bad decisions that we have made over the course of our lives. Unfortunately, to add insult to injury, certain consequences cannot be avoided. However, if we trust God and truly repent, I am confident that he is able to redeem the time in our lives, and cause supernatural acceleration. I speak from personal experience. That said, back to my lottery example.

The next day as the winning numbers are announced, you discover that your ticket contains all of the winning digits. Congratulations!!!! You're a multi-millionaire!!! But wait! Your checking account still shows the same balance from yesterday. You live in the same house, and you still drive the same car. So what changed? May I submit to you the only thing that has changed in that very moment is the information you received? Do you remember our conversation just after we both purchased our tickets? We talked about all of the things we dreamed about doing if we won. The information you have just received about your winning ticket has moved you from at state of hope to a state of expectation. You can now confidently demand a multi-million dollar payout because you now have the evidence of the winning ticket to back up your expectation. You have new information that directly connects you to a new expectation, and your exposure to this new information has produced a new faith image deep within you. All of the things you talked about doing can now be your reality, because you are armed with new information. You start to internally interact with those things in your imagination, which causes faith to explode within you. You now have a different perspective and new outlook on life. Before you even receive the first check, you have already made plans to spend the money. Your actions have aligned with your expectations, and you have officially moved into a new realm of faith based on these expectations.

This shouldn't be so difficult to imagine. Most of us engage in this same exercise in faith the day before payday. Before we receive that direct deposit into our bank accounts, we already know how much to expect, what bills are to be paid, what groceries we need, and if we will have enough to finally purchase those new shoes. In fact, our expectation is so firm, if something happens to go awry with our paycheck, I have no doubt there would be consequences and repercussions. We do not just hope to get paid; we EXPECT to get paid. This is how expectation differs from mere hope.

Expecting God

Approaching God can be a daunting undertaking. I think

most of us can agree that prayer is the fundamental method to approaching God. However, this sparks more questions regarding our approach. How long should we pray? Is God even listening to us when we pray? What if we run out of things to say while in prayer? What should we even expect from such an awe-inspiring, Almighty God? These are the types of questions that plagued me as a new believer learning to seek God. I received Christ when I was thirteen years old, and I knew very little about how to pray or how to interpret scriptures properly. As you would imagine, I struggled to gain even a modicum of confidence in my walk with God from a practical perspective. In addition, I grew up in a very legalistic church that often misinterpreted what it took to have an authentic relationship with God. I witnessed the havoc that erroneous preaching and teaching wreaked on the hearts of sincere seekers. More emphasis was placed on the types of clothing one should wear rather than how to engage in life-changing, transformative communion with God. All I knew was I needed to be saved so I would not die and go to Hell. That was it. I was told to just repeat the "sinner's prayer" and hope to one day speak in tongues, which was the only evidence signifying the baptism of the Holy Ghost, and I would be Heaven bound. I pictured God as this invisible being far away that was quick to punish me and hesitant to bless me. Quite naturally, I had a tough time seeking God because my perception of him was totally off. Not until years later did I realize that God was nothing like what I originally perceived him to be. Fortunately, God allowed me to cross paths with godly men and women who were gifted to articulate to me what God was really like. This truth interrupted the pattern of my erroneous thinking, and birthed within me a true hunger and thirst for the living God. Through these godly relationships, God began to reveal his true nature to me. Ironically, this forged within me an insatiable desire to know more about him. Many times we think God is strictly punitive in his interactions with us, but this is far from the truth. There are times when he does chasten us, but his correction is always steeped in love. Jeremiah 31:3 (KJV) states, *"The LORD hath appeared of old unto me, saying, Yea, I have loved thee with an everlasting love: therefore with lovingkindness have I drawn thee."*

The first order of business as we approach God in prayer is to settle in our hearts that he absolutely loves spending time with his children. We must arm ourselves with the light of his word concerning who he is, and be fully convinced of the nature of God as it relates to how he interacts with his children. Part of the reason why people have a difficult time praying is because it goes against the grain of our carnal nature. Our flesh hates to pray because prayer does not make sense. Logically, prayer seems like a waste of time to our flesh. Think about it. Why should a person steal away all alone, and spend time talking to an invisible being? These types of thoughts stifle our every effort to commune with God on a higher level, so we must arm ourselves with the word of God in order to defeat these adversarial thoughts.

The word of God supplies us with the weapons that we need to blast through enemy ranks and break through to the reward of God's presence in prayer. God welcomes us with open arms whenever we come to him in faith. This is perhaps the greatest privilege of knowing him. In the words of the beloved poem written by Joseph M. Scriven, that later became the famous hymn, *"What A Friend We Have In Jesus"*:

> *"What a friend we have in Jesus*
> *All our sins and griefs to bear*
> *What a privilege to carry*
> *Everything to God in prayer"*

God desires to be with those that expect and desire to be with him. We will always be challenged to carve out quality time to spend with God if we do not expect him to meet us in a very tangible way. Remember, expectation breeds preparation. Our actions in preparing to seek God reveal our expectations as we approach him. So, what does that look like?

When we approach God in prayer, it requires us to be open to whatever he wants to say to us in that moment, like empty vessels expecting only to be filled with him. In essence, to expect God is to release all assumptions of who we think he should be. God is not like us, so we can never fully understand him. We are incapable of knowing how God will answer us, but we must still expect him to answer. This places us in a very vulnerable position, and this is the foundation of our dependence upon him. This is the definition of trusting God. Interacting with God requires trust. Part of the awesomeness of who he is resides in the fact that he knows each of us intimately, and his interactions with us are uniquely ours. Think about how we interact with other people. No two interactions are the same. We are complex, multifaceted beings, and each of our relationships reflects that truth, and our relationships with God should be no different. Like any other relationship, spending time with that person is paramount if we are to really know them. What we experience in our time with God is directly proportionate to what we expect to receive in his presence. If we expect little, we will receive little. If we expect and prepare to receive much, we will inevitably receive much. This should be the cornerstone of our time with God. Again, God desires to be with those that desire and expect him. Remember this one simple truth, God only reveals himself to those who avail themselves to him. Preparation is a huge component to availing ourselves to the presence of God. Simply setting a time to meet God, and keeping that appointment, reveals our heart and positions us in faith to receive what God has for us. Hebrews 11:6 (KJV) states, *"But without faith it is impossible to please him: for he that cometh to God must believe that he is, and that he is a rewarder of them that diligently seek him."* Faith provides us with the internal image of God waiting for us when we start to pray. This image should excite us and ignite a fire of anticipation deep within our hearts for the presence of the living God. One of my favorite scriptures to meditate on as I prepare for prayer is James 4:8 (KJV*), "Draw nigh to God, and he will draw nigh to you…"* Setting a prayer appointment, and keeping it, is a practical way to fan the flames of expectation. The more time we spend in prayer, the more sensitive we become to the voice and the wisdom of God.

To make this practical, I always bring a pen and journal with me into my prayer time each morning. God often speaks to me using parables and illustrations. I love being outside in nature because I view it as God's pulpit. He speaks to me concerning spiritual things through the lens of biology. I never know when God is going to speak concerning something that I have observed or read about in my past, so I arm myself with a pen and paper to capture what he tells me in those moments. This does require a level of patience when seeking him, because not every prayer session is filled with God speaking. I will not go into detail concerning the many different types of prayers that we can employ, just know that God understands our needs before we approach him. Sometimes, I pray for specific things, then there are times when I simply worship without asking for anything at all. Sometimes, I just need to vent to God about how I am feeling in that moment, then there are times when I am silent, and I simply bask in his presence. Part of expecting the presence of God in our prayer time is simply extending to him the invitation to just be God.

Unrealistic Expectations

Not long ago, after completing an online order, a confirmation email was sent to me with a link to retrieve a tracking number for my delivery. I love tracking numbers, because they allow me to see exactly where my package is in the delivery process from the warehouse to my house. I felt great about my order and my expected delivery date. Each day I would check my tracking number to ensure everything was still on schedule to arrive as expected. Again, I did not just hope to receive a package, I was expecting it. At the time, I was living in an apartment complex, so I placed a delivery note within my order to leave the package with the office staff instead of on my doorstep. The day that my package was scheduled to arrive I was excited, and I continued to track my delivery throughout the day. Once I received confirmation that my package had arrived, I couldn't wait to get home to rip into it. When I finally got home, and checked with the office staff, I was perplexed to find that there was no package. I checked the confirmation email again that claimed the package had been delivered, but it was not there. Disappointed, I called the delivery company to see if someone had made a mistake. To my surprise they could not locate my package. I eventually called the manufacturer and requested a full refund. To this day, I believe someone manipulated the system and made off with my order.

Sometimes, we experience disappointments when it comes to our expectations. Remember, the quality of information we consume influences our expectation, so it is extremely important to reconcile what we see, hear, and feel with the truth of God's word. I was disappointed because my tracking information led me to expect something that was not there. Unfortunately, in this instance, the information I had received from my tracking number was erroneous, leading to disappointment.

This is an illustration of what has happens in our church culture. There has been an onslaught of erroneous information concerning God and the Bible. It is difficult for the average person to determine what is true or error, leading to an epidemic of apathy and hostility toward God. We are holding God to an unrealistic standard, expecting him to do things he never promised us he would do. We are uninformed, misinformed, and altogether confused about what to expect in our pursuit of God. As a result, we are quick to believe what we hear instead of doing our homework and experiencing God for ourselves. This is why it is imperative to connect with a church that is teaching sound doctrine based on the truth of God's word, so that we can skillfully assimilate it into our daily lives. It also behooves us to behave like the Bereans in Acts 17 who "searched the scriptures daily" to ensure we understand the relevance of God's word and its application in various situations.

Fortunately, God wants to lead us into what is true and good for our lives, so he has given us his tracking numbers in the scriptures. His Spirit tells us what belongs to us, and his word allows us to track those things right to the doorstep of our lives. It is our responsibility to study the word of God so that we will know what to expect from him. If we do not rightly divide the word of truth (2 Timothy 2:15) by dissecting the meaning and context of scriptures, we will be vulnerable to unnecessary frustration due to our unrealistic expectations. I live by a general rule when expecting from God. If I cannot find at least two contextually sound scriptures to support my expectation, I will defer to God's sovereign will in regards to how he answers my petition, whatever that may be. On the other hand, if I can locate at least two scriptures to support my expectation, I will set my expectation for that specific thing, interacting with it internally until it comes to pass. For example, to expect God to meet us in prayer is totally realistic and encouraged. There are scriptures that support this expectation, and we should fully expect God to meet us in our prayer sessions daily, because this is what he promised to do (Jeremiah 29:12-13).

Promise vs. Principle

As it relates to our study of the word of God, it is important to note the subtle differences between a promise and a principle. I have witnessed so many people struggle with the disappointment that comes from expecting God to do something he never promised to do. I have even been guilty of this myself. One of the hardest lessons I ever had to learn was how to tell the difference between a promise and a principle when studying God's word. Let's examine and contrast the two now.

Promises

The canon of the Holy Scriptures is a fishbowl of sorts, because we get to analyze, examine and interpret the successes and failures of God's people, as the details of their lives are spilled onto the pages of the Bible. We are quick to dissect the actions of others when we study biblical narratives as if we would have made better decisions when placed in those same situations. We get to view the Scriptures from an aerial view, and lay claim on any promise that sounds exciting to us, not taking into account the context of what we are reading. In a general sense, context speaks of the time and setting in which the scripture unfolds. In order to engage with the Bible hermeneutically, we must interpret the chapters and verses through the lens of proper context. God's word is filled with promises, but not every promise is meant to be claimed by us. For example, when God promised King Solomon riches and wealth in 2 Chronicles 1, it was within the context of what King Solomon had previously asked for… wisdom and knowledge to lead and govern as king. Does this mean that if we ask God for wisdom and knowledge today, that he will automatically give us riches and wealth? I'm afraid not. This specific promise was made to King Solomon for a specific reason. In fact, God promised to make Solomon the richest, wealthiest, and wisest king ever because of the colossal task that he was assigned to, and because of the promise God made to his father, David (1 Kings 9:5).

A promise is defined as a legally binding declaration that gives the person to whom it is made a right to expect or to claim the performance or forbearance of a specified act (Merriam-Webster Dictionary). A promise can only be considered a legitimate promise if the person who makes the promise has the ability to perform it. Furthermore, only the person(s) to whom the promise is made has the right to expect what was promised. This is the foundational truth to understanding in regards to what to expect from biblical promises.

When reading the Bible, we have the luxury of peering into the lives of the patriarchs and matriarchs of old as they interacted with God. This privilege of theological "eaves dropping" on conversations had between God and his people can be a double-edged sword when viewing the promises of God through the lens of biblical exegesis. We must exercise caution when interpreting the promises that God made to others in scriptures, and always remember they are made to specific people, for specific reasons, and for specific seasons. Just because we can locate a promise in the Bible does not mean we have the right to claim that promise for ourselves.

Say for instance, you want to reward your child for making all A's in school. One day you decide to go to her school while class is in session. You walk through the door of her classroom, where you see her sitting with all of her classmates and teachers. You point her out and commence to making an announcement in front of the entire class. Your announcement is a promise to your daughter that if she makes all A's, you will take her on a trip to Disney World at the end of the school year. Everyone who hears your promise celebrates with your daughter. Fast-forward to the end of the school year and your daughter has worked very hard, "kept the faith" and made all A's. Now it is time for you to deliver on your promise. Suddenly, you receive a call from your daughter's best friend stating that she wants to claim her trip to Disney because she also made all A's. She states that she should receive the same trip you promised to your daughter because she was in the classroom on that day, and heard you make the promise. Does she have a right to be angry when you say "NO?"

When we claim certain promises in the Bible, we sometimes fall into this same trap. Just because we have access to read all of the promises of God in the Bible, does not mean we should expect those promises to happen for us. We get angry with God when he says "no" or "not yet" because of our erroneous expectations.

The Three C's of Promise Interpretation

We often choose random scriptures and try to turn them into promises in an attempt to force God's hand to perform for us. This is usually a set up for major disappointment, but the good news is…there is a better way. There are actually some amazing promises that we can hang our hats on that are designed especially for us. But first, we should do our due diligence before we expect to receive anything from God. We must understand the context of the promise; the continuity of the promise; and the conditions of the promise. I call these the 3 C's of promise interpretation.

Context

Understanding the context of a promise demands that we

know the setting in which the promise was originally made. This involves knowing the cultural framework in which God was speaking at that very moment. What were the major events happening during that era? Who was God specifically speaking to when he made the promise, and why did he make that specific promise in the first place? What was going on in the life of the person(s)? How did God fulfil his promise to that person? By studying the context, we get a much clearer picture regarding how we should interact with that particular promise. This also gives us the confidence to move in faith as we claim a particular promise. Context helps increase the intensity and clarity of our internal faith image. When we fully understand the original intent surrounding the promise and its implications, it gives our expectation a foundation upon which to rest.

Continuity

The continuity of a promise refers to its congruency throughout the entire canon of scripture. There should always be multiple scriptures to support what we are expecting God to do. If you cannot find at least one to two additional scriptures to support your claim, more than likely that promise is not intended for you. In the book of Exodus, God promised Moses an opportunity to see his glory (Exodus 33:1-34:35). God promised to meet Moses at a specific time in a specific place on Mount Sinai to give him a replacement pair of tablets containing the Ten Commandments. Though I am utterly fascinated by this interaction between God and Moses, it would be silly for me to expect this same type of visitation from God just because I read it in the Bible. This promise lacks the continuity needed for me to claim it for myself. This is the only instance in scripture that God interacted with a man in this manner. I am not saying it is impossible for God to ever interact with me in this manner. What I am saying, is there simply is not enough scriptural evidence to move me from mere hope into full expectation that God would meet me at the top of a mountain somewhere, and literally pass by me in all of his glory. What I can expect from God is wisdom, direction, and internal peace when I pray. There are countless scriptures to support my expectations of these things in my life, and these are the things that I spend my energy pursuing.

Conditions

When studying the Bible, we discover there are two different types of promises. They are unconditional and conditional. Unconditional promises are those things that God has determined to do which require nothing from us. These are the things that God does simply because he is good. There is no action required on our part for us to experience the benefits of what God has determined to do. The next time you happen to see a rainbow in the sky, I encourage you to pause and thank God for his unconditional promise to never flood the entire Earth again like he did in Noah's day (Genesis 9). We did nothing to inherit the benefit of that promise, yet God faithfully keeps his word.

Conversely, conditional promises carry an associated stipulation, or condition, before the benefits are released. As in my previous example regarding the daughter who made all A's, if the condition is not met, the reward is forfeited. These are the "if-then" statements that we see in scripture. Quite often, these types of promises require a certain threshold of action and, in most cases, a waiting period between action and manifestation. For all intents and purposes, we will name this threshold of action the "activation energy." Every conditional promise requires us to do something specific to qualify for the manifestation of that promise. When we release the activation energy required to qualify for the promise, we position ourselves to see what we are believing God for. We must then be willing to wait for the season of manifestation without losing the sustained effort required to birth what we are expecting. This entire process requires faith.

When God first reveled himself to Abraham (Abram) he was 75 years old. God promised Abraham and his wife, Sarah, a child, and commanded them to relocate. Upon obeying God, Abraham released the activation energy required to see that promise manifested, but he still had to wait for the right season. It was not until 25 years later that Abraham and Sarah had their promised child, Isaac, together. All the promises of God are for specific reasons and seasons, and many of them require patience before manifestation is realized. The author of Hebrews said it best, *"And we desire that every one of you do shew the same diligence to the full assurance of hope unto the end: That ye be not slothful, but followers of them who through faith and patience inherit the promises,"* Hebrews 6:11-12 (KJV). The conditional promises of God are designed to not only comfort us, but to also change us. As we maintain consistent action through the waiting period before manifestation, we are actually transformed by the process. This is the power of God's promises.

Principles

Unlike promises, principles are accessible by everyone, regardless of race, background, gender, moral integrity, etc. In my opinion, principles are a more solid foundation upon which to build expectation. Think of principles as laws that govern the operations of life. Simply put, a principle is defined as a comprehensive and fundamental law, doctrine, or assumption (Merriam-Webster Dictionary). Principles are neutral. They are neither good nor bad. They are simply the underlying reasons why certain things consistently happen. Promises usually require the human will to be fulfilled. Principles do not. Promises can be easily broken, principles usually cannot. They happen automatically, and will work for anyone who employs them independent of our will. They work the same way for all.

Principles can be best understood by examining natural laws, such as gravity. For instance, the principle or law of gravity works the exact same way every time, by pulling everything towards the center of the earth. Gravity engages everything in the earth that has mass in the same manner. It matters not if you are a man or woman; 10 pounds or 210 pounds; a hummingbird or a lion; a ship or a car. Gravity is the fundamental law that pulls things toward the ground. There are some instances when we need to be engaged by gravity...like when we are on a roller coaster. In this instance gravity can be our friend. However, there are times when gravity is not so friendly...like when we inadvertently miss a step and engage in intense fellowship with the ground. In both situations, the same law applies. We are being pulled to the ground by the same principle that is always active and ready to engage us. In one instance, we have prepared ourselves to be engaged with gravity in a way that is exciting and fun. In the other instance, we have not, which could very likely result in serious physical harm. The difference is in how we interact with the law of gravity.

There are countless principles in the Bible that are designed to teach us how life works. Once we engage these biblical principles, they will bring about specific results in our lives as we align ourselves with the outcomes that we desire. The book of Proverbs is a gold mine as it relates to biblical principles. King Solomon spent a large part of his life observing and documenting these principles so that we could learn wisdom and govern ourselves accordingly. One such principle is the dangers of laziness. Let's take a look at this principle together.

"I went by the field of the slothful, and by the vineyard of the man void of understanding; And lo, it was all grown over with

thorns, and nettles had covered the face thereof, and the stone wall thereof was broken down. Then I saw, and considered it well: I looked upon it, and received instruction. Yet a little sleep, a little slumber, and little folding of the hands to sleep: so shall thy poverty come as one that travelleth; and thy want as an armed man,"
Proverbs 24:30-34 (KJV).

Contained in these verses is one of the most clearly stated principles in the Bible. This principle brings to light the fundamental connection between laziness and lack. Before we start to dissect this principle for study purposes, please note that the word "lack" in this sense is not just referring to financial resources. Laziness opens the door to many types of lack in our lives. Lack of quality relationships, lack of energy and motivation, lack of opportunity, and the list goes on. It is definitely possible to miss out on opportunities due to a lack of drive and hard work. A slothful person is one who puts forth little to no effort or work to better themselves; one who abhors action and ambition. To be fair, there are various factors that may contribute to poverty and lack. From oppression to physical handicaps or disabilities, lack can be brought on by things that are out of our control. King Solomon was out on a stroll one day and came across a vineyard. Based on his observation, he was able to connect a spiritual principle to his natural observation. The vineyard was overgrown with weeds and thorns. The wall was crumbling and falling down creating a terrible eyesore. From this simple observation, King Solomon saw a spiritual principle in operation before his eyes. What he documented confirmed that laziness is the killer of productivity, and slothfulness opens the door to lack. Like King Solomon, we must learn how to observe and consider. This is a very important skill to develop when seeking to apply biblical principles. The reason why principles are so powerful is because they consistently produce the same results, giving the observer the opportunity to predict a certain outcome. This is why in my opinion, principles are superior to promises when it comes to establishing realistic expectations.

When studying the principles in God's word, we learn a little more about what to expect when we make certain decisions. Principles have already been set into motion, so all we need to do is learn the principle and move into action according to that principle. The force of the underlying law will take care of the rest. If you want to reap the benefits of the principle of friendship, be friendly. If you want to reap the benefits of the principle of prosperity, start investing and giving. If you want to be closer to God, simply start spending more time with him. Just like gravity, these principles are always in operation and ready to engage whoever will yield to their power. They flow in a certain direction, like rivers, and if you jump in and yield to the currents, you will automatically be swept up, so choose wisely which principles you employ.

Conclusion

God has promised us marvelous things in his word. However, we must diligently study the Bible to properly distinguish which promises are available for us to claim as our own. God has also set into motion powerful principles that allow us to observe patterns and, to a certain degree, predict outcomes. This in turn gives us the necessary faith to confidently expect God to behave in a certain manner when we employ these spiritual principles. James 4:8 states that if we draw nigh to God, he will draw nigh to us. This principle gives us boldness to approach God in prayer expecting him to engage us based on our faith in him. Using this one simple principle, we have the confidence necessary to move from mere hope to expectation as we prepare to interact with the Almighty God.

CHAPTER 4
S.P.E.A.R.

Align with God's Will (The Transformation)

"And be not conformed to this world: but be ye transformed by the renewing of your mind, that ye may prove what is that good, and acceptable, and perfect, will of God," Romans 12:2 (KJV)

Please allow me to pause for a moment to say thank you if you are still reading this book. It really means the world to me that you have chosen to take this journey with me. I do feel the need to insert a disclaimer here. Please be forewarned...the contents of this chapter are extremely heavy. An integral part of my healing process has been total transparency. I realize the next few pages will not be very pleasant reading, but if you choose to continue walking with me on this journey, I hope it will be therapeutic for all of us. That said, let's carry on, shall we?

For over six years, I was furious with God. From around 1999 to 2005, I lived my life in a state of perpetual anger, because I blamed God for the terrible condition of my life. At that time my marriage was failing, I had just lost my job at a large telecommunications firm, and death had become a frequent and unwelcomed visitor as several of my loved ones passed away. I felt as though I was a prisoner in my own mind as I tried to make sense of all the terrible things that were happening to me.

I grew up in a church that taught me being born again came with certain privileges. If I "lived right" God would answer all of my fervent and sincere prayers because I was special to him.

No one prepared me for the times when God chooses to say "NO." What happens when it seems like God has turned a blind eye to your prayers and fasting? What happens when your faith stops breathing? What happens when death ignores you when you speak in tongues, and you find yourself looking down at the casket that holds both your loved one and your faith? Does God cease to be good? What is our response when our will and God's will face off on the battlefield of life? Who wins?

When we learned my aunt had cancer, my entire family was shaken. Though it shocked us, we knew God could heal her. After all, we were the family that prayed together. Literally, we gathered as a family to have prayer and Bible study on Saturdays to just bask in the presence of God. It was amazing. To us, God was greater than cancer. As my aunt started treatments, we remained hopeful through the process that God would come through with a miracle. The cancer was of unknown origin which happened to manifest in her lungs. She was young, beautiful, and she loved God. She never smoked and was always glowing with positivity. I knew this was just an attack from the enemy and was confident that God would win by manifesting complete and total healing for his glory. As time passed, there were moments of victory and struggle. The roller coaster of emotions was dizzying, but we all kept the faith. As we came together as a family to pray, we trusted God for her healing in spite of the doctor reports.

Eventually, the cancer began to tighten its grip, mercilessly stripping away both her hair and her weight. I will always be haunted by the images of my aunt being ravaged by coughing spells that shook her entire frame. As she sat up in her bed trying to catch her breath after every cough; eyes watering, and knees drawn into her chest, I remember asking, "God, why are you taking so long to heal?" My will and God's will were engaged in an epic battle. I wanted my aunt to be healed and live, and

God wanted my aunt with him living in the blissful freedom of Heaven. Like sands falling through the neck of an hourglass, I felt my faith slowly dripping away with every cough. Day by day, the coughing worsened until eventually, there was no strength left in her body. As her coughing gradually grew silent, my image of a powerful and loving God began to slowly decay.

When I received the call that my aunt had passed away, I had no words. I was speechless. I didn't know how to process what had just happened. At that moment, something in me cracked like glass just before it shatters into a million pieces. I did not understand why God had chosen to take my aunt in spite of our fasting, prayers, and confessions of healing. All of the tough questions began to flood my mind, and started to slowly harden my heart like drying concrete. God, what did we do wrong? Did we not pray enough? Did we not fast enough? If you didn't heal my aunt, how can I ever trust you to do anything else? What was the purpose of all of this anyway, and why should I pray for anything else? As I earnestly sought answers to these questions, God was painfully silent.

In the days that followed, I found myself quietly embracing the pain that these unanswered questions perpetuated within me. With each passing day, my pain turned into despair, despair turned into apathy, apathy turned into anger, and anger turned into defiance. I was angry because the only person who could explain why I had lost my job, my marriage, and my aunt in spite of my prayers stood silent. In my mind, God was just sitting back watching this tragedy play out, and doing absolutely nothing to help me. I felt betrayed by God, and during that time, my pain was screaming louder than God was speaking… so I released my grip. I yielded to the voice of the enemy that was puppeteering my pain. First, I stopped attending church, because church people began to really annoy me. The overwhelming pain and unanswered questions drove me into a life of rebellion against God. I found that most of the people in church were just going through the motions without any real conviction. When I opened up to express what I was feeling, all I got was the same religious hyperbole that frustrated me even more. All of it was just empty words and expressions that meant nothing to me anymore. I felt as though there was no reason for me to continue going through the motions, so I stopped. From there it became easier and easier for me to sleep in on Sundays, especially after being out in the club the night before. Filled with pain and unanswered questions, my mind became the perfect breeding ground for agnostic ideologies. Just for clarification, agnostics believe the existence of God is unknown and cannot be known. They neither claim faith or disbelief in God. They live under a giant question mark as it relates to the existence of God. This is where I found myself, as I struggled with extreme doubt and depression. Losing my aunt was definitely the proverbial straw that broke the camel's back, leading me into one of the darkest seasons of my life. I later learned, however, that this was not the end of my aunt's story. I will share what helped me see her death from a different perspective a bit later in this chapter. For now, let's take a closer look at how God chooses to express his will.

God's sovereignty forces us to come to terms with our own frailty. When we find ourselves blinded by the limitations of our humanity, it can be extremely difficult to align with God's will. This is partly because of our limited field of vision. We can only see so far down the road. If we are to know God in his essence, we must embrace our frailty as human beings living under his almighty sovereignty. What makes God supremely sovereign is his inability to be anything other than who he is. This is one of the laws of logic called the Law or Principle of Identity. He is wholly God through and through. He can be nothing else. He has nothing to prove, because he is the standard. He measures himself by himself because there is none greater, and according to one of my favorite scholars, Ravi Zacharias, he exists because he can't NOT exist. He is GOD! One of my favorite scriptures is Hebrews 6:13-14 (KJV), *"For when God made promise to Abraham, because he could swear by no greater, he sware by himself, saying, Surely blessing I will bless thee, and multiplying I will multiply thee."* When God speaks, it automatically becomes truth, because he cannot perform in any way that is not congruent with who he is. That said, who God is ultimately defines his will, because he has no reason to be anything other than who he is and will always be. We can either align with his will and abide in his peace, or resist his will and endure a life of toil independent of his grace and help.

Trusting God and yielding to his will is not always easy. In fact, sometimes, it is downright brutal. When Jesus was in the garden of Gethsemane shortly before his death, the agony of alignment was evident. In Luke 22, Jesus was in agony as he petitioned God to remove the cup of suffering from him that he was about to endure. There in Gethsemane, we see an epic clash of wills as Jesus struggled to align with the will of the Father. Fortunately for us, Jesus quickly submitted to the will of the Father, endured the cross, and purchased our salvation through his death, burial, and resurrection. If Jesus found himself engaged in a battle of wills, where does this leave us with our sinful natures as we attempt to align with God's perfect will? We absolutely cannot accomplish this feat apart from a living connection with the Father. We must consistently find ourselves in the face of God as we navigate the labyrinth of life.

It becomes a little easier to submit to the will of God when we settle once and for all that he loves us like no one else can. God's love is relentless, and cannot be compared to anything in this limited sphere of our understanding. His love is simply incomparable. The closest thing that we have to understanding God's love is a mother's love for her children. Think back to when you were young, and wanted your mom to buy you a new toy, or a sweet treat, or take you somewhere new and exciting. When mom said "yes"--oh the joy and anticipation that followed. How about those times when mom said "no?" Do you remember how you felt? I sure do. The disappointment was almost utterly unbearable. Our immaturity severely hampered our ability to understand why the answer was "no." Our limited knowledge of the family finances, or the potential dangers of certain activities narrowed our scope of understanding regarding why "no" was best for us at that time. What we wanted and what our parents wanted could not coexist in harmony at that time, so we had to submit to the "no" if we knew what was best for us. This is how we must approach God in prayer. Ravi Zacharias speaks of how we sometimes approach God in our prayers, *"The first mistake we make is to turn prayer into merely a wish list because when those wishes aren't granted, we struggle to believe in God and feel that he has disappointed or failed us."*[6] God is not a genie, and we must be prepared for his "no" if we are to align with his will.

The Triune Will of God

God's will is more complex than any of us could ever imagine. Many of the things that we may desire for ourselves may not be the things that God desires for us. Conversely, some things that God may allow in our lives are things that we would have never chosen for ourselves. We may not fully understand the why behind God's will, but he has given us a glimpse into how his will influences his behavior. In Romans 12 we read: *"I beseech you therefore brethren, by the mercies of God, that ye present*

---

6. Ravi Zacharias, *Has Christianity Failed You?* (Grand Rapids, MI: Zondervan, 2010), p. 160.

your bodies a living sacrifice, holy, acceptable unto God, which is your reasonable service. And be not conformed to this world: but be ye transformed by the renewing of your mind, that ye may prove what is that good, and acceptable, and perfect will of God," Romans 12:1-2 (KJV).

Here we see the triune will of God expressed as good, acceptable, and perfect. We may not know the will of God at all times, but our duty as his children is to trust him. Part of the fallacy of being angry with God is the belief that God has somehow ceased to be good. Remember, God does not change because it is not necessary for him to change, and this triune expression of his will is a reflection of his nature. He is good... what he does is acceptable...and he is perfect. He has always been who he presently is, and he will always be who he has always been. To know God is to trust that he is, and always will be good. Everything that he allows or prevents, he does so because he is completely good. The problems we encounter regarding God's will is never with his goodness, but rather our lack of understanding. We can never know as God knows, because we will never be able to see as God sees. Let's take a closer look at these three expressions of the will of God.

God's Will is Good

When seeking God's will in any situation, it is imperative to first settle in our hearts that God wants what is best for us. This is not just a cliché; it is a fundamental truth. Despite the circumstances that life will inevitably bring our way, we must magnify the fundamental truth that no matter what, God is supremely good. What he does is eternally connected to who he is. God's will for our lives should never be viewed through the lens of an isolated event, whether perceived as good or bad. I always remind myself to not judge any situation as good or bad until enough time has passed for me to realize how that situation has shaped my character. Situations themselves are neutral. They are neither good nor bad. When it comes to any situation in our lives, it is not about how we feel in it, but rather who we become because of it. God's will does not always feel good, but it always works for our good, because God is all good.

God's Will is Acceptable

As we spend more time with God on a daily basis, we become more mindful of his love and presence around us. One of the benefits of increased awareness is a greater sense of peace. In fact, the peace of God is like our spiritual compass. The Bible teaches us in Isaiah 55 that one of the results of seeking God and calling upon him is the compass of peace. *"Seek ye the LORD while he may be found, call ye upon him while he is near; For ye shall go out with joy, and be led forth with peace...,"* Isaiah 55:6,12a (KJV). Never underestimate the peace of God that comes from being in his will. Whenever I have tough decisions to make, I rely heavily on what gives me the greatest peace. One of the meanings of the word "acceptable," according to Strong's Concordance, is to be "fully agreeable." So when we bring this meaning into the context of God's will for our lives, we discover that what God wants for us is ultimately what we desire anyway. Being connected to God brings his will to light into our lives. This is another fundamental truth. When we pray fervently and sincerely, our wills become intertwined with God's. In essence, God becomes the one who causes us to desire what he desires. Prayer produces within us the God perspective. We begin to see how he sees and desire what he has already desired for our lives. Paul teaches in Philippians that God gives us the desire to do what pleases him. *"For it is God which worketh in you both to will and to do of his good pleasure,"* Philippians 2:13 (KJV). God does the work when we present to him an available vessel. He carries out his acceptable will in our lives, and the more we yield to him, the more agreeable his will becomes. The more we seek God, the more we realize his will is specifically tailored to us, and in most cases, it is what we have longed for all along.

God's Will is Perfect

Lastly, God's will is perfect. This is the expression of God's will that most reflects his nature. The word perfect simply means "complete." God is not stressing out about what is going to happen next. Nothing takes him by surprise. That means whatever he allows or prevents, he has already observed the end result of that specific occurrence, and has made provisions to be glorified in it. The perfection of God in this case refers to the completeness of his omniscience. He knows what is going to happen this time tomorrow. For this reason, it behooves us to allow him the luxury and space to be God. Not only is his knowledge perfect, but more importantly, his love towards us is perfect. We must learn how to trust him even when he says "no" or "not yet" remembering God's "no," quite often means he sees bigger and has better for us.

Being a manager at a large healthcare organization, I see this truth play out daily. When senior leadership makes decisions, often they are made based on a level of understanding and foresight that the average employee is not privy to. Some decisions seem to contradict common sense at that moment. However, if the leadership is savvy, time will reveal that those decisions were indeed sound ones. This is how God's will functions in our lives. We may not understand what God is doing in our lives in the moment, but time always reveals that he is a good, good Father who knows how to take care of his kids.

When I was about 11 years old, I learned the hard way to trust my parents when they said "no." One day after school, I wanted to ride my bike around the neighborhood. When I asked my mom, she paused and said, "no." She told me that she had a bad feeling about me riding that day, and she didn't want me to ride. Of course, I was disappointed and started to pout. My will and my mom's will were in conflict at that moment. As an immature child, I did not understand what my mom meant when she told me she had a "bad" feeling about me riding my bike. Seriously, what was so bad about a simple bike ride? I was so angry, frustrated and disappointed with my mom for forbidding me to ride my bike. I begged and begged and begged until she eventually gave in despite her initial hesitation and allowed me to ride. I was so excited to finally get what I wanted; I immediately pulled out my bike and took off. While on my ride, as I was coasting down a hill, a car made a left turn and slammed into me as I was riding through an intersection. The impact knocked me off my bike, up into the air, and I came crashing down head first on top of the car, then onto the asphalt. I was immediately knocked unconscious, and to this day, I don't even remember the impact. When I regained consciousness, I was lying on the ground with a crowd of people standing above me. My mom, dad, and sister were all frantic among the crowd. I remember my mom taking me in her arms and praying life over me. She declared then and there that I would live and have no broken bones in my body. As I was in and out of consciousness, I remember her telling me to confess with my own mouth that I was going to be OK. She kept telling me to speak it. I was so out of it, I vaguely remember mustering up the strength to confess that I was going to be OK. Once I confessed it, I was out again. The next time I regained consciousness, I was inside an ambulance on my way to the hospital. Thank God there were no broken bones just like my mother declared. Needless to say, I should have listened to my mom that day when she said "no."

Many times we ask God for things that are not good for us at the moment of our request. When we do not receive the answers that we want, we get angry and pout because God is saying "no." We fail to realize that God's perspective is light years beyond ours, even when it comes to our own lives. One of my favorite scriptures is found in Isaiah, *"For as the heavens are higher than the earth, so are my ways higher than your ways, and my thoughts than your thoughts,"* Isaiah 55:9 (KJV). God's perspective is eternal. He abides in eternity and observes time from that perspective. Since he dwells in eternity, he has already observed everything that happens and will happen to us. So he knows what we can never fully know. So when he says "no" or "not yet," he is operating from a place of love and mercy because he sees how it will affect our future. Since God manages the affairs of the believer from his position in eternity, he is the only one qualified to be fully trusted with our lives. He sees the end and the beginning in the same glance; therefore, he is able to declare what will happen in the end. He is not bound by time, so he can be fully trusted. Isaiah 46:9-10 (KJV) states, *"Remember the former things of old: for I am God, and there is none else; I am God, and there is none like me, declaring the end from the beginning, and from ancient times the things that are not yet done, saying, My counsel shall stand, and I will do all my pleasure."* Because God sees the effect that our requests will eventually have on us, he longs to give us what is best for us. If we are convinced God is good when we receive what we ask for, then we must also believe this truth through the dark seasons of our lives when he doesn't answer the way we think he should. Even when the answer is "no" or "not yet," it is imperative that we trust God, and open ourselves to receive his better plan for our lives. Our greatest pain is experienced when we try to place God in the box of our limited perspectives. Our faith in God's love for us should never be predicated on the outcome of any temporal experience or situation. Of course this is easier said than done. Building a strong relationship with God requires learning how to manage the paradox that sometimes presents when interacting with him. Let us now examine this paradox a little closer.

The God Paradox

Life in Christ is fraught with contradiction. The type of contradiction that can sometimes cause us to question what we really believe. Honest Christians will readily admit that part of walking with God is learning how to wade through the waters of paradoxical experiences to reach a level of homeostasis in our faith. Living in this state of paradox requires the skill of walking the tightrope between confidence and uncertainty; blindness and belief; strength and vulnerability without wavering. In fact, the tightrope that we rest the totality of our lives upon is our faith in Christ. Paul described this lifestyle best in Galatians when he penned, *"I am crucified with Christ: nevertheless I live; yet not I, but Christ liveth in me: and the life which I now live in the flesh I live by the faith of the Son of God, who loved me, and gave himself for me,"* Galatians 2:20 (KJV). In this passage, we find the perfect example of the Christian paradox. Notice Paul's language here in this verse, *"I am crucified, nevertheless I live."* These contradictions frequently frame the Christian life creating an environment that forces us to live in a state of perpetual vulnerability.

A paradox is essentially a truth that seemingly contradicts common sense, but yet remains true within the parameters of a certain context. For example, when looking at the menu at a seafood restaurant, one may noticed a paradox of sorts when ordering jumbo shrimp. Of course, we all know that there is nothing "jumbo" about shrimp, however, when comparing jumbo shrimp to other normal-sized shrimp, this becomes true within that context. This brings to light a particular problem when applying this same concept to the truth of God's nature. As we grow in Christ, we are forced to negotiate the terms of our faith in God when we encounter these paradoxes. In fact, faith itself is a paradox. Learning how to "look at" the "unseen" and act upon it is difficult to do at times, but it is paramount when pursuing God. We cannot please him unless we learn how to embrace the paradox that is in him. Hebrews 11:6 reminds us that without faith, it is impossible to please God. When we are faced with difficulties, sometimes it is challenging to see the "goodness" of God in the "badness" of our circumstances. It can sometimes feel like God is so far from us, yet in Hebrews 13:5, he said never leaves us nor forsakes us. We even get a glimpse of this paradox as Jesus was on the cross. In Matthew 27:46, Jesus cried out with a loud voice, *"My God, my God, why have you forsaken me?"*

When I was entertaining agnosticism, the paradox that fueled my confusion was that of the goodness of God. If God is good by nature, then why does he allow bad things to happen? Many atheists and agnostics hang their hats on this one argument for disproving the existence of God. I even embraced this argument as a way to deal with the anguish of the excruciating grief that I was going through when I lost my aunt, my job, and my marriage. Because I could not properly trace the goodness of God in the midst of my pain, I erroneously made him the author of my pain. Agnosticism was a natural outgrowth of my pain produced from the dissonance caused by this irreconcilable paradox (the goodness of God vs. the badness of my circumstances). Because God was not "behaving" like I thought he was supposed to, I questioned his existence. I began to doubt everything from the goodness of God to the love that I once experienced in his presence. What started out as disappointment grew into full-blown misery and hopelessness. The fire of hope that once animated my life was slowly being reduced to a flicker as disappointment after disappointment crashed over me. I vividly remember going on a job interview for a great paying job with amazing benefits that would allow me to get back on my feet. I was able to interview with the hiring manager at the time, and established a wonderful rapport with him almost immediately. After the interview, I was so excited. I felt my hope building once again. Weeks went by with no calls and no job offers. I finally called the hiring manager only to learn that the company was in a hiring freeze, and was possibly about to experience another round of layoffs. The Bible mentions in Proverbs 13:12 how *"hope deferred makes the heart sick."* My heart was definitely sick from the roller coaster ride of exciting ups and disappointing downs.

When God Dies

The agony of the God paradox can leave us feeling confused and frustrated as everything around us appears to die. Can you imagine what the disciples felt when they witnessed the unthinkable…Jesus bleeding to death on Golgotha? After all of the miracles and wonders they saw him perform, and even worked alongside him to assist as two fish and five loaves of bread turned into baskets of leftovers after feeding thousands of people… THOUSANDS!!!! Imagine being on your boat when Jesus literally shows up walking on the water, then invites you to do the same. Imagine being caught in a hurricane on the sea, as your boat is about to capsize, then watching Jesus wake up from a nap and command the storm to cease…and it stops in its tracks. Imagine what it must have felt like to witness a dead man named Lazarus wake up from a four-day deathly slumber to be restored to full vitality as if death never even happened. Imagine witnessing all of these things with your own eyes, then with those same eyes witnessing the death of the man who did all these things, claiming to be the Son of God. I can only imagine what was going through their minds as Jesus was beaten, spat on, and publicly humiliated as he traversed the Via Dolorosa en route to Golgotha to die. I would definitely have some tough questions swirling around in my head at that moment:

"Why is Jesus just standing there saying nothing?"

"Why won't Jesus just FIGHT BACK?"

"Why won't he transfigure himself like he did that time on the mountain? Then they'll see that he really is the Son of God!!!"

Of course these questions are easier for us to manage today because we know that Jesus was indeed resurrected with all power, and now sits at the right hand of God. Unfortunately, for the three days that Jesus was in the tomb after his death, the followers of Jesus did not have this luxury. To them, the Son of God was indeed dead. How could this happen? Jesus was dead. All they had invested, was now gone down the drain. The time they spent away from their families doing ministry, feeding the hungry, healing the sick, teaching and training… all in vain. Jesus was dead. He could have easily summoned his angels to rescue him at any moment, but he didn't. He could have thrown down that cross and escaped into the crowd while on the Via Dolorosa, but he didn't. He could have done any number of miracles to save himself from this plight, but he didn't. Instead, he chose to tap out to death. What a paradox it was when the Son of God died.

Is it so difficult to imagine what they must have been feeling? I think not. In fact, may I submit that we still ask these same questions today, just in different contexts.

"Why won't God heal my body?"

"Why didn't God save my marriage?"

"Why do I keep falling into the same cyclical sin? I know God can take away the desire."

These are the types of questions that plague our generation, and make it challenging to pin down what the will of God actually is in these situations. So how do we maintain our faith and weather the storms of life when these contradictions come crashing in? One way is to seek God's plumb line.

The Plumb Line

When I was a teenager, my dad decided to tear down our old collapsing deck in the backyard, and build a new one from the ground up. For me, this was super exciting, and I could not wait to help with this project. We were like Chip Gaines from the HGTV show *"Fixer Upper"* as we tore down the deck on demo day. That was the fun part. Once we finished demolishing the old deck, it was time to get serious. My dad and I meticulously measured every piece of wood before cutting and placing them into their respective places. Dad's mantra was "measure twice, cut once." In other words, be absolutely certain the measurement is correct, because when the sawing starts there is no turning back. In many ways, I still live by this mantra today.

One of the many tools my dad introduced me to was the chalk line. This was a unique instrument used to establish a perfectly straight line between two points to ensure a straight cut. It was easier to cut in a straight line when following the chalk mark left on the wood. Each piece of wood we cut fit perfectly in place because we "measured twice and cut once" using our chalk line as the source of truth when cutting.

Similarly, another instrument used as a source of truth in measurement is called a plumb line or a plumb bob. Plumb lines use gravity to establish a true vertical when building. A specialized weight is attached to a heavy duty string, and is designed to hang free creating a perfectly straight vertical line. In order to ensure the walls and doors in a structure are perfectly vertical or "plumb," professional builders often use plumb lines to ensure the integrity of the entire building. Can you imagine what would happen if one wall was not perfectly vertical while building a house? The end result could be disastrous. There must be a source of truth for us to reference as we build from God's blueprint for our lives. This source of truth is the voice of God. God's voice is the vehicle that he uses to communicate his will to us, so it is paramount that we consistently connect with him in prayer to hear what he has to say. Our time with God creates the true vertical whereby we measure our alignment with his will. In all transparency, discerning the will of God is not always easy. Many times, it requires making some adjustments in our lives. Aligning with God's will may sometimes mean sacrificing our pride on the altar of God's sovereign desire for us and others.

I promised before I ended this chapter I would share how God helped me through the darkness. Just like I experienced a series of painful events that caused me to question God's love and existence, I also experienced a series of miraculous events that totally changed my life. A considerable time after my aunt passed, I was having a conversation with my mom, who was there with my aunt as she was transitioning to Heaven. She began to share with me some astounding information regarding what she witnessed one day while visiting my aunt. While there in her room, my aunt awoke from sleeping and began speaking with my mom. She asked my mom "Where is that music coming from?" My mom recalled there was no music playing in the room at all. When she asked my aunt about this music, she told her it was the most beautiful singing she had ever heard. She asked my mom, "Don't you hear that choir singing?" My mom told her that she didn't hear anything. Then my aunt gasped and said, "Look at all of these lights. This place is lit up like Las Vegas!!!" It was then that my mom realized my aunt was experiencing Heaven. Her spirit was flying between the two realities of Heaven and Earth. A few days later, she transitioned to that beautiful city of lights. What bliss she must be enjoying now. The reason why I believe in God is because my experiences make it difficult not to. Living my life in relationship with him is the only way I have been able to make sense of life. Some swear by science, which is one's own prerogative. I've found that science has its place in explaining the "what" and to some degree the "how," but it can never explain the "why." I've experienced God's love and I am persuaded that to know him is to be loved by him.

God desires to expose us to marvelous things that we have never seen or experienced before in him. However, our fallen, sinful nature creates in us a bending or a proclivity to drift away from God's divine plan for our lives. When our finite minds cannot understand or ascertain what is happening all around us, we sometimes falter in our faith. Our comfort zones can lull us into a deep slumber causing us to drift ever so quietly away from God's best for our lives. It is in these moments that it becomes necessary to make adjustments if we expect to hit our target and fulfill our destiny.

I once heard a talk by U.S. Astronaut, Scott Kelly, in which he recounted his one-year mission to the International Space Station in 2007. He mentioned how important it was to never lose focus on the task at hand. Kelly stressed the necessity of continually making tiny adjustments called course corrections during his journey to land on the Space Station as it orbited roughly 250 miles above Earth. In many ways, this principle also applies to our daily lives. This is why prayer is so vital to our mission to accomplish the will of God for our lives. Our perspective regarding the events of our lives naturally become distorted due to our sinful natures, but as we pray daily, God is able to correct us and realign our wills to his as our hearts soften in his presence. Ravi Zacharias described it this way:

> *"Prayer is hard work. Being aligned with God's will is no light matter. For Jesus, just at his most desolate and agonizing moments, even as he faced the agony of being separated from his Father to make it possible that we would never have to face that total abandonment, he was, in fact, right in the center of his Father's will."* [7]

Conclusion

As we seek God and align with his plumb line, the Holy Spirit initiates subtle course corrections that keep us in vertical alignment with his will. As we faithfully abide in God's presence, he projects the image of his will upon our hearts, and little by little we are transformed into the image of Christ. It is how we come to know God the way he originally intended to be known. In essence, time with God is the currency of transformation and through our alignment with his will, he rewards us with the glory of his presence.

7. Ravi Zacharias, *Has Christianity Failed You?* (Grand Rapids, MI: Zondervan, 2017), p. 166.

CHAPTER 5

S.P.E.A.R.

Release the Love of God (The Fruit)

"But the fruit of the Spirit is love, joy, peace, longsuffering, gentleness, goodness, faith, meekness, temperance: against such there is no law," Galatians 5:22-23 (KJV)

According to BlueLetterBible.org the word "LOVE" appears in the Bible 310 times. Suffice it to say, love is the cornerstone of the Christian faith. In fact, it is virtually impossible to sail the waters of Christianity without the wind of love. It is the foundation upon which the entirety of the gospel rests. The Christian faith elucidates both the veracity and the tenacity of God's love for man. *"For God so loved the world, that he gave his only begotten Son, that whosoever believeth in him should not perish, but have everlasting life," John 3:16 (KJV)*. Upon this foundational scripture sits the glorious Gospel of salvation. The fact that he loves us is amazing, but how he loves us is literally mind-blowing. God's love is the only force that is capable of changing the human heart, because he is the only person who truly understands the heart of man. Hebrews 4:12-13 (KJV) states: *"For the word of God is quick, and powerful, and sharper than any twoedged sword, piercing even to the dividing asunder of soul and spirit, and of the joints and marrow, and is a discerner of the thoughts and intents of the heart. Neither is there any creature that is not manifest in his [God's] sight: but all things are naked and opened unto the eyes of him with whom we have to do."*

Because of our human nature and the sin in us, one would think God, in his infinite omniscience, would have absolutely nothing to do with us. Yet, he chooses to chase us down relentlessly with his love. For those who have sincerely experienced the love of God, the transformational effects are undeniable and contagious.

Love: The Fruit of Christianity

Love should be a natural outgrowth of the Christian life. When the Bible speaks of the nature of love and what it produces in us, in many cases it draws a comparison to how trees produce fruit. Growing up in the Deep South, I am very familiar and fascinated with farming. My summers as a child were spent on my grandparents' farm in Alabama, where I witnessed the wonder of watching fruits and vegetables grow before we harvested the bounty. It takes diligence and patience to reap a harvest. Sowing and reaping is much more than just digging a hole in the ground and throwing in seeds. Consistent watering and weeding must accompany sowing if a successful harvest is expected. Different seeds require different timeframes and conditions to produce. Once the right conditions have been met and the plant matures, it will automatically begin releasing its fruit.

In much the same way, when we encounter the love of God, he plants the seeds of his love deep within us. We become like the fruitful trees mentioned in Psalms 1:3, bringing forth fruit in the appropriate seasons of life. One of the most powerful teachings of the biblical outgrowth of love is when Jesus himself instructed his disciples to love one another at the Last Supper as recorded in John 13. Jesus explained what was expected of all his followers after his death, which was quite simply to reproduce what had already been planted within them. *"A new commandment I give unto you, that ye love one another; as I have loved you, that ye also love one another,"* John 13:34 (KJV). Here,

Jesus mandates with a commandment the directive to love each other. The picture of an investor comes to mind as Jesus elaborates on his example of love. As Jesus had invested in his disciples day after day during his tenure with them, he demanded a return on that investment by commanding that they invest in each other in the same way. The currency used in this divine investment is love. Its value is so immense, that Jesus declared it to be the royal diadem of our sacred faith. The love that we wear and release to others on a daily basis is the most demonstrative sign of a true follower of Christ. It is the fruit that hangs from our lives to feed the starving masses. *"By this shall all men know that ye are my disciples, if ye have love one for another,"* John 13:35 (KJV). Remarkably, the defining characteristic that denotes our connection to Christ is love. Not if you have tons of money, or if you attend church, but *"If ye have LOVE one for another."* Our connection to Christ produces very specific qualities in our lives that are not only experienced by us, but also visible to others. Galatians gives us a robust list of qualities that should adorn our lives as seekers of Christ. Love is so significant to our Christian life and to God, we find love sitting in the number one spot among the fruits of the spirit, *"But the fruit of the Spirit is love, joy, peace, longsuffering, gentleness, goodness, faith, meekness, temperance: against such there is no law,"* Galatians 5:22:23 (KJV).

The qualities listed above are only produced to the degree that we are connected to Christ. Trees don't "try" to grow fruit; the presence of fruit just happens if the tree is healthy. The branches upon which the fruit hangs must meet one substantial prerequisite. They must remain connected to the actual trunk of the tree. I know this may seem elementary, but its practical application in our lives may prove to be a bit more daunting. In order to produce the highest quality spiritual fruit, we must remain connected to Jesus in our daily devotion, seeking him with our whole hearts. When we spend time with God, ponder His

Word, expect His presence, and align with his will, in time we will begin to see these characteristics and qualities showing up in our lives. Things that once pressed our hot buttons, causing a reflex response, may not affect us in the same negative ways as we mature.

In no way am I making the case for an easy journey. The work of staying connected to Jesus can mean heavy lifting at times. Loving difficult people takes Christ. Finding joy in the mundane and painful experiences of life can pose a challenge from day to day. Let's not even talk about the "L" word—LONGSUFFERING! Just looking at the word "longsuffering" conjures up feelings of dread in my mind. Fortunately, Jesus never intended for us to make a go of this life alone. He promised to be with us in the form of the paraklētos (Strong's G3875)…the Holy Spirit himself. Our responsibility is to remain connected to our Helper at all time using the paradigm that I have set out in this book as a tool. As branches, if we remain faithful in our love and worship of the Father, the principle of fruitfulness will inevitably manifest its power in our lives. In one of my favorite verses, Jesus stated how this principle of fruitfulness works: *"Abide in me, and I in you. As the branch cannot bear fruit of itself, except it abide in the vine; no more can ye, except ye abide in me. I am the vine, ye are the branches: He that abideth in me, and I in him, the same bringeth forth much fruit: for without me ye can do nothing,"* John 15:4-5 (KJV)

With any command that we observe in scripture, the power to perform it is innately contained therein. Jesus gives each of us the power to remain in him. In this chaotic world full of distractions and noise, it behooves us to set our minds to do the work of abiding in him via daily prayer and scriptural study and affirmation.

Love: The Engine of Faith

Now that we have examined the effects of love on us, let us now focus our attention on the effects of love as it relates to those we come in contact with. We understand that love naturally exerts its force in and through us as part of our connection to Christ, but what happens when that force is observed and experienced by others? I would argue that the results are transformative. In fact, if we profess Christianity in truth and sincerity, then we are the product of another person's fruitfulness and obedience. Proverbs states, *"The fruit of the righteous is a tree of life, and he who is wise wins souls,"* Proverbs 11:30,(NASB). The salvific work of Christ is rooted in love and faith. In order to influence our generation, our platform must be love. God's desire and design for true salvation is for everyone to have a living experience with him that changes the heart. This experience often comes through the witness of a life that has not only been affected by the love of Christ, but is available to release and perpetuate this same love to affect others. This is the whole point of it all. It is why we teach Christ "and him crucified" (1 Corinthians 2:2).

Faith in Christ is one of the only vehicles that brings authentically radical and lasting change. What makes the vehicle of faith so unique is what's under the hood, so to speak. *"For in Jesus Christ neither circumcision availeth any thing, nor uncircumcision; but faith which worketh by love,"* Galatians 5:6 (KJV).

Faith is only faith when it is living and active. When I was a child, I would dream of one day being able to drive. I would ask my parents if I could sit in the driver's seat and pretend to speed down the highway while the car was parked. It was exhilarating just to grab the steering wheel with both hands and make engine noises with my mouth as I imagined driving off into the sunset. If there is no corresponding action animating what we label as faith then it's like sitting in the driver's seat making engine noises with our mouths going nowhere. Love is the engine of faith. It's what causes faith to move into action, and without it, we are just making noise. The Apostle Paul penned it perfectly stating: *"If I speak with the tongues of men and of angels, but have not love [for others growing out of God's love for me], then I have become only a noisy gong or a clanging cymbal [just an annoying distraction]. And if I have the gift of prophecy [and speak a new message from God to the people], and understand all mysteries, and [possess] all knowledge; and if I have all [sufficient] faith so that I can remove mountains, but do not have love [reaching out to others], I am nothing,"* 1 Corinthians 13:1-2 (AMP).

I fear that we have lost touch with the miraculous because we have lost our compassion for others. Pain has become so pervasive and ubiquitous; our hearts have grown cold and numb to the plight of our brothers and sisters. Our own selfishness has made our hearts callous and insensitive as we pass by hurting people each day. People all over the world are in inconceivable pain, and everyone is looking for an exit. The tragic truth is many people do not know how to access true transformation, so they settle for a slow, comfortable death. If we are to be a catalyst for transformation in someone else's life, transparency and compassion are the prerequisites.

The word "compassion" connotes a strong feeling of sympathy and pity according to Vine's Expository Dictionary. To further reinforce this truth, as Matthew's Gospel records the miracle of multiplication when Jesus blessed the two fish and five loaves, preceding the miracle, we see Jesus being "moved with compassion" (vs. 14) just before he miraculously healed and fed the multitude. The love that Jesus had for people was so strong, it "moved" him to act, and the results were literally miraculous.

The flame of love toward God has dampened within us causing our vision to become dim. When we fail to see and identify with the pain of others through God's eyes, we lose the ability to be fruitful for the Kingdom of God. In order for most fruit bearing trees to remain fruitful, at some point, they must undergo the process of pruning. Cutting away the old, unproductive branches that no longer yield quality fruit is essential to a healthy tree. I remember being shocked as a child seeing this process play out. At first glance, it seems to be a brutal undertaking as the branches are stripped away leaving only a skeleton of a tree. However, as seasons pass, new branches begin to grow and eventually produce loads of healthy fruit...even more than in previous times due to the pruning process. In like manner, our hearts must undergo a spiritual "cutting away" in order to maintain fruitfulness and sensitivity to God and his people.

In the same vein, the word "covenant" actually connotes the process of cutting according to Vine's Expository Dictionary of New Testament Words. Whenever God extended his reach to man throughout the Old Testament, he often established an agreement or a covenant to bring about salvation and wholeness to the world. To enforce the terms of said agreements, God would require bloodshed through sacrificial cutting. It was always a gruesome scene that signified the gravity of what was being established between Heaven and Earth; between God and man.

Possibly the most famous covenant recorded in the Bible was between God and Abraham, when God required Abraham and his sons to be circumcised in order to enforce the terms of the contract establishing Abraham as the father of many nations (Genesis 15).

"It was the flesh of the foreskin that was to be cut off, because it is by ordinary generation that sin is propagated, and with an eye to the promised seed, who was to come from the loins of Abraham. Christ having not yet offered himself to us, God would have man to

*enter into covenant by the offering of some part of his own body,
and no part could be better spared. It is a secret part of the body;
for the true circumcision is that of the heart..."*

Thank God for the perfect work of his dear son Christ that
shed his innocent blood to satisfy the terms of the New Covenant under which we now live. As part of our covenant with
Christ today, we must still submit to the surgical precision of
God's blade as he cuts away the foreskins of our hearts along
with the unproductive branches of our lives. Pure, unadulter-
ated love is the engine that propels us to sacrifice our wills and
agendas for a greater good. Until we walk in true love, we will
never know what it is to offer up our hearts through circumcision to fulfil our part of the New Covenant; to love others
as we love ourselves. I love how the TANAKH (New Jewish
Publication Society Translation) translates Jeremiah 4:3-4, *"For
thus said the Lord to the men of Judah and to Jerusalem: Break
up the untilled ground, and do not sow among thorns. Open your
hearts to the Lord, remove the thickening about your hearts..."*
Only when we actively cut away the thick, impenetrable places
of our hearts and open ourselves to the love of God, will we be
able to be sensitive enough to be moved by the pain of others
again. God is able to make our hearts compassionate to others
as we spend more and more time in his presence. Once we feel
what God feels, and see how he sees, we can then move into action and respond to others how he would respond to us in our
times of need. The engine of love and compassion will ignite
our hearts and put our faith into motion setting the stage for
the miraculous.

Love: The DNA of God

Television talk show host, Maury Povich, has built a prominent reputation proving paternity (or the lack thereof) of hundreds of families as he famously announces "You are/are NOT the father!!!" The suspense before each announcement is both maddening and addictive. Paternity testing is based on comparing the genetic DNA of two individuals to prove parentage. The genetic material of both parents is combined to form a new cell. This is the beginning of a new life, uniquely different, but closely related.

Our Heavenly Father created us in his image and after his likeness to represent him in the earth. He is our Holy Father... uniquely different from us, yet closely related to us. When we are born, I believe we arrive with an innate longing to reconnect with him and to feel the sense of unique spiritual belonging that only he can provide. There is an undeniable yearning deep within us that calls to us throughout our lives. This yearning is often misinterpreted by many, and suppressed by others, but the presence of his DNA in us can never be denied. We are his creation and his seed of love in us can never die. Before we understand it we long for it. John Calvin first coined this longing as the "sensus divinitatis" or sense of divinity.[8] Before we realize what it is, we search for it. We are drawn to it even when we try to escape it. To know God is to be loved by him, and in turn to fall in love with him. The oneness that is felt when we are in true relationship with God is the primary benefit of seeking him. We become conjoined with him at the heart like Siamese twins, sharing in his joy and at times feeling his grief. His DNA in us makes us his sons and daughters. For this reason, it escapes me when I observe people who say they know him yet their overall disposition is nasty, cold, and miserable. As followers of Christ, our default disposition should be love, *"Beloved, let us love one*

---

8. James K. Beilby, Thinking About Christian Apologetics: What It Is and Why We Do It, (Downers Grove, IL: InterVarsity Press, 2011), p. 144.

another: for love is of God; and every one that loveth is born of God, and knoweth God. He that loveth not knoweth not God; for God is love," 1 John 4:7-8 (KJV). I seriously question a person's relationship with God if the top fruit of love produced by his indwelling spirit is lacking. When we accept Christ as Savior, he changes the internal physiology of our spirits. We function totally different as a result of his presence within us. Take a look at this scripture, "*Therefore if any man be in Christ, he is a new creature: old things are passed away; behold, all things are become new,*" 2 Corinthians 5:17 (KJV). In Christ, we are changed into a new species of sorts. Not like an alien or anything, but more like a new version of ourselves. God replaces the engine that moves us. He replaces the engine of selfishness and carnality with one of love and compassion. When we embrace our newness in him, we began to resemble him in more ways than one. Our Father bestows upon us his very nature through the genetic material contained within the blood of Jesus is Son making us long to be like him in every way.

Conclusion

Love is one of the most powerful forces in existence. To have access to the source of love through spiritual rebirth and daily sanctification is in itself a miracle. As we join ourselves to the heart of God through prayer and worship, we are exposed to the power that transforms us from slaves to sons. May we allow God entrance into our hearts and by the power of the Holy Spirit release the force of God's love into the world as we accomplish our mission to expand his Kingdom.

CHAPTER 6

S.P.E.A.R.

The Battle Plan

"Beloved, now are we the sons of God, and it doth not yet appear what we shall be: but we know that, when he shall appear, we shall be like him; for we shall see him as he is,"
1 John 3:2 (KJV)

If I had to choose one word that encapsulates what it takes to intimately know Jesus it would be diligence. It takes a persistent, tenacious hunger for God to push through the resistance and distractions that are designed to thwart our godly exploits while discovering who Jesus is. There is no cookie cutter formula for getting to know him, because he tailors his love to each of us individually. How God interacts with you is totally different than how he interacts with me. What may be an obstacle or weakness for you, may not be for me or the next person. This is what makes our relationships with him so beautiful. We are his sheep, and he knows us better than anyone else. As we spend more time with him, we begin to see things in a totally different light. However, there are times when certain obstacles may get the best of us as we grow into mature seekers.

In an effort to capture this beautiful diversity, I solicited the help of some of my very close friends to gather data that may be helpful for new seekers on their journey to deeper intimacy with Christ. I formed a small focus group to discuss and uncover some of the major challenges and obstacles one may encounter when learning how to seek God, and how to overcome those challenges. In this chapter, we will examine those obstacles and pose some helpful solutions based on the information discussed in our focus group. The group consisted of people all of whom have been born again ten years or longer. With that in mind, let's dig in.

Three Keys to Supernatural Growth

As I gathered and analyzed all of my findings from our group, I noticed that some common themes began to emerge. The following five items were posed to the group for discussion:

Please briefly describe your first encounter with God.

1. Please briefly describe your first encounter with God.
2. How did your life change after that encounter?
3. What advice would you give to someone struggling to understand how to seek God?
4. What obstacles do you face when you approach God in prayer?
5. How do you overcome those obstacles?

After compiling all of the answers, I was able to extract three things that mature believers do in order to consistently maintain a strong relationship with Christ. They consistently immerse themselves in prayer (seek), they consistently exercise obedience to God (submit), they consistently engage in kingdom work (serve).

Be Immersed in Prayer (Seek)

Mature believers cherish God's presence in prayer. There really is no getting around this one. Every single person in our focus group expressed an intense commitment to prayer. Not just occasionally saying grace over their food, but the type of commitment that gently nudges them from their sleep early every morning to spend time with God. Why prayer? Because once a person has seriously tasted the presence of God, nothing else in this world compares. Mature seekers understand the importance of daily prayer. Without it, our hunger for God gradually wanes until we find ourselves drifting...carried away by the currents of apathy. Prayer produces a craving for the presence of God that only grows the more we pray. That is simply the way God designed it, and the responsibility lies upon us to cultivate our prayer garden each day to experience the fullness of God's presence. Thoughts can sometimes spring up in our prayer time like weeds in a garden. Don't fret, this is normal. We have the power to arrest every wayward thought and cast it away as we pour out our love on the Father in prayer. What a privilege!

Exercise Obedience (Submit)

I will be the first to admit, obeying God is not always a walk in the park. The friction between flesh and spirit is ever-present within each of us, creating a challenge each time we seek to obey God. Paul said it best when he penned, *"And I know that nothing good lives in me, that is, in my sinful nature. I want to do what is right, but I can't. I want to do what is good, but I don't. I don't want to do what is wrong, but I do it anyway,"* Romans 7:18-20 (NLT).

This friction, though ever-present, can be overcome, and victory can be gained by exercising the muscle of obedience. The more we yield to and act on the promptings of the Holy Spirit, the easier it becomes to recognize when God is directing us. For anyone just starting on this journey of knowing Jesus, it may seem daunting at first. It may not be clear what the first steps should be. How do I know when God is speaking to me? What does God's presence "feel" like? How long should I pray, and what do I say? All of these questions are very common. In describing their first encounter with God (question #1), members of our focus group reported truly experiencing God only once they decided to fully surrender to Jesus and accept him as Savior. One member of the group was a very young five years old when she received Jesus and was shortly thereafter baptized with the Holy Spirit. She recounted that as she continued to seek God, the voice of God became increasingly clearer. One of her more vivid experiences was when the Holy Spirit spoke to her one day as she was leaving her grandparents' home in New Jersey. As she was putting on her seat belt, she heard the Spirit tell her that would be the last time she would see her grandfather. A few months later, he fell ill and passed away. Today, she serves as one of the lead intercessor at our church.

Spiritual growth and maturity don't just haphazardly happen. It hinges upon our ability to recognize and obey the promptings of the Holy Spirit. Time with God and taking risks to step out on faith to obey when he speaks to us creates the conditions for supernatural encounters with God. The more we train ourselves to listen to the voice of God and move on what we hear, the more he shows himself strong on our behalf. Is this easy to do? Not at first. It takes trusting him over time, and once those muscles are developed, we become a force to be reckoned with.

I vividly remember one night, in my college days at Alabama State University, a group of us had gathered together for our weekly campus ministries Bible study. One of the young ladies in our group walked in and began to complain of a sore throat and laryngitis. Her voice was severely hoarse, and she was in pain. Immediately, I felt the prompting of the Holy Spirit to pray for her. Admittedly, I was a bit nervous at first, but I decided to ask her if I could pray for her. She consented. I laid my hand on her throat and prayed for her to be healed. When the prayer was done, I told her to speak, and immediately, her voice returned and she was instantly healed. All praises to God!!! Did that happen because I was such a powerful Christian? I'm sure we all know the answer to that question. Of course not! In fact, I didn't know what was going to happen when I prayed for her. All I know is, I believed the prompting I sensed was from God as I heard the Spirit tell me to pray for her, so I obeyed. He did the rest. This is all God asks of us. Just trust and obey me, and he will do the rest.

Engage in Kingdom Work (Serve)

The Kingdom of God has an economy all its own. Not only do we get to serve God and express our gifts and talents for the furtherance of the gospel, but we get to witness other people's lives changed by the power of God. Mature seekers embrace their dual citizenship, and consistently sow their time, talents, and treasure into the kingdom of God to catalyze change in others. R. Kent Hughes states:

"Big hearts, the enlarged hearts that God uses, are laboring hearts which, though weary, will willingly be expended as necessary. You may fancy that you have a ministering heart, but if you are not laboring for the gospel in that place where God has put you, and do not find yourself being inconvenienced by your commitment, you are deluding yourself."[9]

Our service is our worship. The heart to serve stems from a clear understanding that we all were once far from God, and if not for him sending someone to cross our path to share the gospel with us, we would still be lost and without hope. When we come together and assemble to work toward a common vision, it causes our hearts to expand and we become the hands

---

9. R. Kent Hughes, *Disciplines of a Godly Man,* (Wheaton, IL: Crossway, 1991), p. 215.

and feet of Jesus. Our capacity to love, and to be loved, grows exponentially when we serve. We were never designed to live in isolation. The weapons of the enemy are most effective against us when we live in isolation. After my divorce, I withdrew from as many public interactions as I could because of the pain. I became a hermit of sorts because of the embarrassment. I did not want to be hurt again, and in my mind people were guilty until proven innocent. I had an unhealthy paranoia whenever I thought about being in large crowds. My overall outlook was grossly negative because I had closed myself off from the rest of the world by putting up these huge walls. Sure, no one could get in to hurt me, but on the flip side, no one could get in to love me. It wasn't until I gained the courage to break down the walls and begin serving others that my pain began to dissipate. This is when my life began to change, and my heart began to heal. I'm still on the road to complete and total healing, but I know through God's ever-present love, I will win.

Avoiding Pitfalls (My Solutions)

Through the help of the Holy Spirit, we are able to communicate with the Father and fellowship with his presence in the fullness of joy. However, this does not come without significant and substantial resistance. Here, I will seek to shed some light on the various pitfalls that are commonly encountered when actively pursuing God, and provide solutions to help proactively clear those obstacles. Let's begin...

Pitfall #1: Distractions
Perhaps the most common pitfall to making significant progress in our walk with God is the incessant demands of life. If it's not work, it's the kids. If it's not the kids, it's the spouse. If it's not the spouse, it's the dog. It seems as if everything is

demanding our time and vying for our attention. Everything is an emergency...or is it? If our goal is to draw closer to God, we must carve out time to be still before him, free from all distractions and demands. Sometimes it's OK to disappear. Allow yourself time alone with God whatever that looks like for you. If you are not connected to your source, what are you really contributing? What value are you bringing to the table if you are spread too thin? I've been there. It is paramount to take care of yourself, and part of that process is spending time with the Creator to be restored. The world strips so much away from. There are times when we do not even realize we are simply running on fumes. Others see it on our faces even when we attempt to hide it.

My Solution: Time Management—I have never been a morning person, but I discovered when I wake up early to pray, it literally places me in a supernatural flow that I cannot find in my own strength. Since I'm not a morning person, it has taken me years to get this one down. I struggled to reconcile what I knew God was calling me to do, and the will to do it. Seriously, I seem to drift into heavenly sleep between the hours of 4:00am-5:00am, and this is the exact time that God requires of me. I used to struggle to get out of bed to meet God in prayer, but once I realized the affect that prayer had on my outlook, I made it a priority. Being a person prone to depression, I was able to cope better when I was obedient and met God early in the mornings. I made adjustments in my schedule and started going to bed earlier to accommodate my time with God. This made it a little easier to get up at 5am. Morning intimacy with the Father became my priority. Take a minute now to think through the best times of day for you to steal away and meet with God. It may be early morning, or late at night when everyone is asleep. It may be in your car during lunch, or while out on an evening walk. The most important thing is to develop a pattern of consistency. This brings me to the next pitfall...

Pitfall #2: Inconsistency

In order to reap the benefits of any discipline, there must be a commitment to growth, and before there is measurable growth, there must be consistency. I have found in my own life experience when I am confronted with intense adversity, my proclivity has been to disengage and quit, causing me to drift from my spiritual fervor. Over the years, I have learned the importance of pressing into prayer and worship with even more intensity during these times. When I was a beginning white belt in Taekwondo, my sensei sat me down and explained the colored belt system to me. Not only did each belt color represent a higher rank, but it also indicated a higher skill level. White belt was the entry level where learning the foundation of form was the focus. Once I achieved green belt, more was expected of me. I could no longer get away with sloppy form. My sensei demanded crisp, quick, and powerful strikes...the type that made the sleeves of my uniform "pop." At this level, I was introduced to live sparring. As I put on my gloves and sparring pads, it was time to put into practice what I had learned as a white belt. However, instead of punching and kicking the air, it was time to actually punch and kick a real person while taking real punches and kicks myself. I quickly learned the value of consistent practice. When I finally achieved my black belt, my sensei sat me down again and had another conversation with me. This time our talk took a deeper and more intense tone. He began to elucidate the deeper philosophies of Taekwondo. He told me that everything I had learned from white belt to red belt was only the foundation. Black belt carried certain responsibilities, and consistency in proper practice became paramount to build effective technique. My fists were no longer just fists...

they were weapons. Form became the foundation upon which the tower of technique was to be built. A tower cannot stand long upon a weak and crumbling foundation. Consistency in doing breeds consistency in being.

The purpose of consistent practice is to build muscle memory so that when the time comes to perform, it is much easier to conquer, and seeking God's presence is no exception. "Practicing" the presence of God is a real discipline. There are certain levels in God that can only be reached by sustained engagement and intimacy with him. Yes, God's grace is there when we fall, but at some point, there must be a "putting away" of things that no longer serve us (1 Corinthians 13:11). If we don't take time to learn ourselves, we will be hard-pressed to know Christ. Paul Pettit once wrote, "Thus, knowing God more deeply cannot be accomplished without simultaneously being willing to know oneself" (Pettit, 2008, p. 128). The "on again, off again" cycle breeds discouragement and frustration. Learning to press in harder when things get tough is an essential skill that is not easily developed. Proverbs 24:19 states, *"If thou faint in the day of adversity, thy strength is small."* The art of consistency in any area boils down to one thing…keep putting one foot in front of the other, and eventually the goal manifests. When we pray and seek God with all our hearts, his presence becomes our goal, and with his presence, he rewards us (Genesis 15:1).

My Solution: Set Goals—We set goals for everything else (career, finances, health, etc.), so why not set goals for our spiritual growth? My recommendation is to start small. I use a daily planner to block my times in the mornings to keep my prayer goal before my eyes. It has been proven that people who create goals and consistently review those goals are more likely to stay motivated to achieve them. Remember, the objective is consistent action. For now, don't worry about the length of your prayer time. Just concentrate on consistently carving out the time to get before God in prayer and Bible reading/study. Your stamina will build gradually as you put in consistent and significant time with God. Move as many obstacles as you can to clear the runway for the Holy Spirit to propel you God-ward. Whatever time you choose, protect that time by anticipating potential distractions and proactively removing them. For instance, if you choose to meet God in the mornings, go ahead and prepare your clothing and food for the next day. Queue up your daily devotional readings, worship music, and other tools to help you connect with God. This will make your life so much easier and take away some of the anxiety the may hinder a productive experience in prayer. Once all the anticipated distractions have been cleared, you're all set to tap into the power of God's presence.

Pitfall #3: Inadequacy

In Luke 11, when one of Jesus' disciples asked for a lesson in how to pray. Jesus laid out the pattern for what we now call the Lord's Prayer. The first two words of the prayer "Our Father..." gives us a glimpse into God's intent as he calls us into intimacy with him. God is our Heavenly Father, and contained within this celestial ascription is the assurance that provides an anchor for our souls. Father (pater-Gk.) denotes "a nourisher, protector, upholder" (Vines Expository Dictionary of New Testament Words). The mangled fabric of our sinful natures has robbed us of the true meaning of what this word really signifies. The eternal God of all galaxies, divine in nature, and omnipotent in his dominion desires to be with us. So much so, that he sent his Son to die so that we would have the freedom to join our hearts to his in covenant and be restored to his image and likeness. The enemy wants nothing more than to wave the flag of our past sins and failures before our faces in hopes to cause us to abort our mission of approaching God. Feelings of inadequacy tend to creep into our minds if there are areas that we have not completely surrendered to God. Intimacy with God is not for the faint of heart. One must be prepared to encounter not only the weight of his presence, but also the depth of our sin. If there is any unconfessed sin in our lives as we make our ascent to God in prayer, it is immediately revealed when the glory of God throws a holy beam onto the landscape of our hearts. This exposure can cause feelings of despair, inadequacy, and even shame. It is during these times that we must focus on who God is, and not on what we have done. The more we bask in the presence of God, the further we distance ourselves from our sinful natures. Remember, he is our Father. He longs to be near us, and he has paved our way to him through the Blood of Jesus Christ. In him, we are enough.

<u>My Solution: Scriptural Affirmations</u>: Part of my prayer experience with God involves taking scriptures into my room and speaking the Word aloud. There are several scriptures at our disposal that we can use to speak over our minds creating a spiritual armor for our minds as we enter into the presence of God. The enemy is relentless, and will use anything or anyone he possibly can to distract and discourage us from boldly and confidently seeking God. My recommendation for silencing the thoughts of inadequacy in your quiet time is to begin by first reading scriptures aloud before you pray. This will initiate the alignment process so that our minds are better equipped to overcome any resistance and receive from God. Here are a few of my favorites:

"Draw nigh to God, and he will draw nigh to you," James 4:8a (KJV).

"If my people, which are called by my name, shall humble them-

selves, and pray, and seek my face, and turn from there wicked ways; then will I hear from heaven, and will forgive their sin, and heal their land," 2 Chronicles 7:14 (KJV).

"It is of the Lord's mercies that we are not consumed, because his compassions fail not. They are new every morning: great is thy faithfulness," Lamentations 3:22-23 (KJV).

"Let us therefore come boldly unto the throne of grace, that we may obtain mercy, and find grace to help in time of need," Hebrews 4:16 (KJV).

"Abide in me, and I in you. As the branch cannot bear fruit of itself, except it abide in the vine; not more can ye, except ye abide in me," John 15:4 (KJV).

"For the eyes of the Lord are over the righteous, and his ears are open unto their prayers: but the face of the Lord is against them that do evil," 1 Peter 3:12 (KJV).

"As the hart panteth after the water brooks, so panteth my soul after thee, O God," Psalms 42:1 (KJV).

"But it is good for me to draw near to God: I have put my trust in the Lord God, that I may declare all thy works," Psalms 73:28 (KJV).

"Thou wilt shew me the path of life: in thy presence is fullness of joy; at thy right hand there are pleasures for evermore," Psalms 16:11 (KJV).

Pitfall #4: Logic

The final pitfall that we will cover is that of our own logic.

This pitfall rose to the surface more than a few times within our focus group. The question asked was, "What obstacles do you consistently face when you approach God in prayer?" Trying to figure out how God is going to fix what is broken in our lives is a very real struggle. Our sinful nature places us in a very difficult position when it comes to trusting God. This epic struggle finds its origins in the Garden of Eden when Adam and Eve ate the forbidden fruit from the tree of the knowledge of good and evil. Man has always desired to not just be "like" God, but in some instances, to "be" God. The enemy knows this about us, and often temps us to forsake the gift of peace and rest in order to attempt to carry our own burdens. When we pray, it forces us to humble ourselves "under the mighty hand of God" (1 Peter 5:6) by arresting our logic and placing us in a posture of submission to his will. None of us truly knows how God is going to answer our prayers when we petition him. It is imperative that we release our preconceived notions and how we think God should accomplish what we are praying for, and honor his sovereignty fully trusting him through the process. We may find that what we are truly praying for is more of his presence to fill the perceived voids that gave birth to the petitions. I have discovered the closer I get to God, the more he satisfies me at my very core. As we replace our own erroneous logic and unrealistic expectations with trust and acknowledgement of God's will, we will find a greater sense of rest, as he directs our lives into his perfect will. Proverbs 3:5-6 states, *"Trust in the Lord with all thine heart; and lean not unto thine own understanding. In all thy ways acknowledge him, and he shall direct thy paths."* Easier said than done…I know. However, once we understand this truth, our own logic takes a back seat to God's superior wisdom.

My Solution: Rest—I speak from a place of personal experience when I say this was a foreign concept to me. Resting in

God should never be confused with slothfulness. Many people use this concept of resting in God as an excuse to veg out on their responsibilities. Not so. There is a prerequisite for rest that must be met before we can claim our portion. The word "rest" as indicated in Scripture denotes a ceasing from labor to regain strength (Vine's Expository Dictionary). If there has been no toil, then there is no need for rest. Many people claim to be "waiting on God" when they have not engaged in any type of labor to catalyze change in their lives. God, in many cases, is "waiting on them."

In regards to prayer, this same concept applies. Labor always precedes rest. When we pray, we engage in real spiritual warfare, fighting real demons and principalities to get to God. This can be very laborious, especially when interceding for others. Resting in God comes as a result of ceasing from the labor of active prayer and transitioning into a place of passive prayer knowing God has heard us, and will answer in his sovereignty in due time. The challenge with finding rest in God is knowing when to cease from labor and accept that God's answer will undoubtedly be for our ultimate good. Authentic, godly rest comes when our worship is never affected by the outcomes of our prayers. After all, we do not worship God for outcomes; we worship to ascribe worth to our Father for who he is.

Conclusion

Embedded within the sovereignty of God is the very nature of God. At its core, the gospel reflects the nature of God through the person of Jesus Christ. If we sincerely desire to know God, we must grapple with the questions that plague our minds, and survey the rugged terrain of our hearts assessing our capacity to desire God's presence more than anything. Only then will the treasures of God's boundless love be opened unto us. Until we are confronted with the abysmal expanse of our sinfulness and truly see ourselves for who we are without God, we will never long for what he has already made available to every human being in existence...a way out. Before you and I were born, the way was already made. God extended his hand, and reached across the canyon of corruption, and sent Jesus to rescue us, because no one else could. You see, he already made the first move, and now he awaits any who will acknowledge that move, and reciprocate in kind. We do not get to set the terms of this contract. We must fully accept and adhere to the terms of this covenant to be eligible to enjoy the benefits of relationship with the sovereign God. To know God is to understand we cannot control him. To know God is to understand his ways are beyond our ability to comprehend. To know God is to live with questions that we cannot answer. To know God is to feel those questions melt away in the fire of his presence. To know God is to:

> S.——Spend Time With God
> P.——Ponder The Scriptures
> E.—Expect An Encounter
> A.—Align With God's Will
> R.—Release The Love Of God

Bibliography

1. Beilby, James. *Thinking About Christian Apologetics: What It Is and Why We Do It.* Downers Grove, IL: InterVarsity Press, 2001.

2. Bland, David Travis. "Real Monsters Charged in investigation of online child predators, Sheriff Lott Says. www.thestate.com/mews/local/crime/article215572485.html: The State, July 26, 2018.

3. Henry, M. "Commentary on Genesis 17 by Matthew Henry." Blue Letter Bible. Last Modified 1 Mar, 1996. https://www.blueletterbible.org/Comm/mhc/Gen/Gen_017.cfm.

4. https://www.addictioncenter.com/nicotine/

5. https://www.drugabuse.gov/drugs-abuse/opiods/opiod-overdose-crisis.

6. Hughes, Kent R. *Disciplines of a Godly Man.* Wheaton, IL: Crossway, 1991.

7. Lewis, C.S. *The Screwtape Letters.* New York, NY: Harper Collins, 1942.

8. Pettit, Paul. *Foundations of Spiritual Formation: A Community Approach to Becoming Like Christ.* Grand Rapids, MI: Kregel Academics and Professional, 2008.

9. Zacharias, Ravi. *Has Christianity Failed You?* Grand Rapids, MI: Zondervan, 2010.

About the Author

Brian L. Evans is a native of Birmingham, Alabama, and now resides in Charlotte, North Carolina. His love for inspiring others through the written word was realized early in his life, and has compelled him to accept the call of God to be an inspirational author. He manages his own blog (Wisdom's Quill), YouTube channel (Brian Evans Unleashed), and is currently working to complete his Master of Arts in Biblical Studies (M.A.B.S.). He loves to read, hike, and ride his motorcycle through the mountains of North Carolina. His mission is to impart the life, love, and power of God into the hearts of all people through written and spoken words designed to produce authentic and lasting transformation.

Brian L. Evans

CPSIA information can be obtained
at www.ICGtesting.com
Printed in the USA
LVHW011056150719
624096LV00002B/178